John G Wilson

The Sabbath and its Lord, and the Divine Man

John G Wilson

The Sabbath and its Lord, and the Divine Man

ISBN/EAN: 9783743351936

Manufactured in Europe, USA, Canada, Australia, Japa

Cover: Foto ©ninafisch / pixelio.de

Manufactured and distributed by brebook publishing software (www.brebook.com)

John G Wilson

The Sabbath and its Lord, and the Divine Man

VOL. I.

DISCOURSES ON PROPHECY.

(SECOND EDITION, INCLUDING THE VINDICATION.)

This is a compendious exhibition, on a scheme entirely new, of the Divine purpose in the redemption of man by Jesus Christ, as revealed in the more sure word of prophecy, which is as a light that shineth in a dark place, showing that the dominion of the world will be given to the saints of God, and that all the rest of mankind will be subject to their government; that in their condition of glory and blessedness the saints will have an everlasting reward; and in their condition of dishonor and shame the ungodly will have an everlasting punishment. But that all sinful intelligences will eventually be subdued and reconciled to God, become obedient subjects of the Kingdom, and, saved from torment and pain, be made as happy as their condition will allow.

In all departments of science new discoveries are considered practicable, and are commonly hailed with delight. Why should not new discoveries in Biblical truth be deemed equally so, and welcomed accordingly? The Bible, as a record of God's thoughts and purposes in relation to the moral government of his creatures, while shedding the dews of salvation abundantly upon thousands of believing hearts and inquiring minds, may have been, like the great book of nature, but partially understood. And the scribe, instructed unto the kingdom of heaven, like the diligent student of nature, is to bring out of this treasury things both new and old. We trust that it will not be deemed presumptuous in us to aim, in humble dependence on God, to fulfil this duty. So far as our knowledge extends, no one else has ever taken the view of the Divine government and proceedings, in whole, which is presented in this volume. Our view, it is true, presents much that is common to all evangelical expositions of the Scheme of Redemption. And where we think we have discovered new light, and have presented new views, we have endeavored to give the reason for the hope that is in us with meekness and fear.

If any one should ask, as some have done, why these things were not discovered previously by the learned and wise and good who have diligently studied the Bible to find the truth? We answer, by inquiring why the circulation of the blood was not discovered before Harvey? and gravitation before Newton? and electricity before Franklin? The Bible is as rich in truth as nature is in fact. In the glorious sky of Revelation, as well as in the natural heavens, there may be stars whose light has not yet reached us, and which may be designed to bless the world in its future track; the discovery of which may be made by some diligent student hereafter. When we consider the dispensations of God as already historically developed or prophetically intimated in his word in their connection with and relation to the great scheme of redemption, we exclaim with Paul, "O the depth of the riches both of the wisdom and knowledge of God! how unsearchable are his judgments, and his ways past finding out,"—and with the Psalmist, "Thou has magnified thy word above all thy name."

We have not the vanity or presumption to suppose that we are above the liability to err; but we have searched diligently after the truth, and have not written a line without conviction of its accordance with the testimony of the Divine word. If we have erred we shall be truly grateful to any one who will point out our errors, and show unto us a more excellent way. We ask a candid perusal of this volume, a thorough investigation of the views of the Scheme of Redemption presented in it, and an unprejudiced judgment respecting them.

We shall be pleased to hear from any who may be interested in our views, and to answer inquiries respecting them. Having derived unspeakable comfort from them to our own mind, we are desirous of communicating the same to others, and therefore invite inquiry and criticism.

May the God and Father of our Lord Jesus Christ, the God of all grace and consolation, grant us the unction from above which shall guide us into all Truth.

(See Advertisement and Notices at the close of this volume.)

VINDICATION.

This contains replies to some notices of the Discourses on Prophecy in which my theory of Redemption was mis-stated, answers to letters, &c. This has been published separately from the Discourses to accommodate those who have the first edition, and will be sent to any one on the receipt of twenty-five cents in money, or postage stamps.

VOL. II.

THE SABBATH AND ITS LORD.

The interest just now awakened in this community on the Sabbath Question, has hastened the publication of this volume, which is designed to supply a need which the author, with thousands of sincere and honest minds, long felt, and which he feels confident he has now reached through a careful and patient study of the Word of God. The reader will, I trust, find a satisfactory answer to the following questions.

Is the Sabbath a Divine Institution?

Is there a moral necessity for it?

Is it of universal obligation?

What was its special relation in the national Covenant made with Israel?

Has the first day of the week been divinely instituted in place of the seventh day, as the Christian Sabbath?—And for what reasons?

How ought it to be observed?—And what works may be regarded as allowable profanations of it?

We invite not only all Christians who observe the first day of the week, but also all those who hold to the seventh day—all Jews, Infidels, and nothingarians, to a candid consideration of the subject here presented, hoping thereby to conduce something towards giving a more healthy tone to public sentiment on this subject, and promoting a more enlightened and conscientious observance of the Lord's day.

To any one who will remit us the price of the book, (75 cents,) it will be sent by mail or otherwise free of expense.

DISCOURSES ON THE APOCALYPSE.

WE hope soon to make arrangements for the publication of these Discourses which are of an expository character, in which every paragraph is separately and explicitly considered, while the most complete and systematic arrangement of the whole is preserved. The arrangement and classification of the Visions presented in this volume will be found entirely new, and we think so natural and harmonious, so consonant with the analogy of faith, and exhibiting the dispensations of God in such agreement with the benevolence and rectitude of his character, as to be commended to the enlightened judgment of all who are in quest of truth. And what has hitherto been regarded by the generality of Christendom as a sealed book, will, we are confident, be made plain to the understanding of the intelligent reader, who will at least, whether he receive or reject our views, have the satisfaction of comprehending our meaning, and being furnished with a key to the interpretation of the symbols by which the agents, acts, and events predicted in this book are represented.

We commit all to the overruling providence of God, and patiently wait for some clear indication of His will, to whom we have consecrated our Writings for the glory of His name—the exaltation of His word, and the salvation of mankind.

THE

SABBATH AND ITS LORD,

AND

THE DIVINE MAN.

By JOHN G. WILSON,

MINISTER OF THE WORD OF GOD.

I WORK FOR GOD AND GOOD.—TUPPER.

PHILADELPHIA:
PUBLISHED BY THE AUTHOR,
AND FOR SALE BY
WILLIAM S. & ALFRED MARTIEN, 606 CHESTNUT ST.
PERKINPINE & HIGGINS, 56 N. FOURTH ST.
1860.

"IN PROPORTION AS THE SABBATH IS IMPROVED, WILL EACH DAY RESEMBLE A SABBATH, IN BEING EMPLOYED FOR GOD, AND SPENT IN THE FRAME OF SPIRIT WHICH MOST RESEMBLES THAT OF THE BLESSED BEINGS WHO KEEP A PERPETUAL SABBATH AROUND THE THRONE."

M. L. D.

"IT IS MANIFESTLY PROPER, THAT BEINGS WHO ARE DEPENDENT UPON GOD FOR ALL THINGS, AND ESPECIALLY FOR THEIR HOPES OF IMMORTALITY, SHOULD DEVOTE A PORTION OF THEIR TIME TO THE EXPRESSION OF THEIR GRATITUDE, AND SUBMISSION, AND REVERENCE.

"COMMUNITY OF DEPENDENCE AND OF HOPE DICTATES THE PROPRIETY OF *UNITED* WORSHIP; AND WORSHIP, TO BE UNITED, MUST BE PERFORMED AT TIMES PREVIOUSLY FIXED."

DYMOND.

Entered, according to act of Congress, in the year 1859, by

JOHN G. WILSON,

In the Office of the Clerk of the District Court of the United States, in and for the Eastern District of Pennsylvania.

CONTENTS.

DEDICATION,	7
THE SABBATH,	8
PREFACE,	9

CHAPTER I.

THE SABBATH, CREATION'S HOLYDAY,	15
Meaning and application of the word,	15
The cosmogony of Moses,	16
The Divine rest,	17
Man not an idler in Eden,	18
The Sabbath not merely to recruit his wasted strength,	19
But to meet the wants of his spiritual nature,	20
And meets a social necessity,	22
The Sabbath a blessing,	23
The first Sabbath in Eden,	24

CHAPTER II.

THE SABBATH, REDEMPTION'S WORKING DAY,	26
Necessary to man before the fall and more so since,	26
I. *The Sabbath before the Law*,	27

CONTENTS.

Known and observed from the beginning,	27
The end of days, Gen. iv. 3, 4,	28
Weekly division of time,	29
Testimonies of Manassah, Ben Israel, and Philo,	30
Observations on Ex. xvi. Gift of manna,	30
II. *The Sabbath under the Law*,	35
Incorporated in the Decalogue,	35
Of perpetual obligation,	37
Promise to Abraham—the natural seed,	38
The Sabbath a sign of their national covenant,	39
Sabbath-breaking a capital offense,	40
National blessings promised,	43
Its aspect to them individually,	47
Its sanctification,	50
III. *The Sabbath under the Gospel*,	54
Result of the trial of the natural seed,	55
No flesh justified by the law of the national covenant,	55
Justification by faith,	56
Object of the gospel dispensation,	57
Observance of the Sabbath not enjoined in the New Testament,	58
Legal aspect of the Sabbath associated with the seventh day rendered a change necessary,	62
The designation of the first day of the week,	63
The first Christians being Jews, kept two sabbaths,	67
Gentile Christians kept but one, and that the first day of the week,	67
Paul would not allow the observance of the seventh day to be imposed on the Gentiles,	68
Inculcated liberty of conscience,	70
The first day of the week the Christian Sabbath,	72

CONTENTS.

CHAPTER III.

THE SABBATH, THE MILLENNIUM'S SYMBOL DAY,	75
Its symbolic character,	76
Adam and Christ—representative men,	77
Work of Christ,	77
Adam's knowledge of the symbolic character of the Sabbath,	79
The Six Days of Creation all symbol days,	79
Tradition of the House of Elias,	82
Paul's argument in Hebrews iv,	83
Testimony of Christian fathers,	86
The Rest remaining to the people of God,	90

CHAPTER IV.

THE LORD OF THE SABBATH,	93
The question, Whom do men say that I am?	93
Humanitarianism,	94
Semi-Humanitarianism,	95
Christ the Son of God,	96
His pre-existence,	98
Personal representative of God,	100
By whom all things were created, etc.,	101
His Incarnation,	102
His unchangeableness,	105
His universal Lordship,	107
Lord of the Sabbath through all dispensations,	108
Lord of the coming Millennial Sabbath,	113

CHAPTER V.

THE OBSERVANCE OF THE SABBATH,	116

CONTENTS.

Man not made for the Sabbath,	116
The Sabbath made for man,	117
Made for man's use,	118
Teachings of Christ: Works of necessity,	119
Works of religious service,	120
Works of mercy,	121
Caution against abuses,	125
Physicians, Apothecaries, etc.,	126
Business on the Sabbath day,	127
Preparation for keeping the Sabbath, etc.,	131
The Millennial Sabbath,	133

THE DIVINE MAN.

DIALOGUE BETWEEN REASON AND REVELATION, etc.,	141
Index thereto,	179

Dedication.

THIS VOLUME

IS RESPECTFULLY INSCRIBED

TO

JOHN CLARK, ESQ.,

Of Baltimore,

AS AN ACKNOWLEDGMENT, BY THE

AUTHOR,

OF HIS ESTEEMED FRIENDSHIP,

GENEROUS SYMPATHY,

AND

TRUE KINDNESS.

THE SABBATH.

Creation's holyday,
   Day of Jehovah's rest,
When ceasing from his finished work,
   His lips pronounced it blest.
Then sang the morning stars,
   Shouted the sons of God,
And man a holy Sabbath spent
   In Eden's pure abode.

Redemption's working day,
   To man in mercy given,
To lay aside his earthly toil
   For intercourse with Heaven:
That shaking off the weight
   Of worldly thought and care,
He may renew his spirit's strength
   In holy praise and prayer.

Millennium's symbol day,
   Type of a rest to come,
When saints, redeemed from sin and death,
   Shall dwell with Christ at home;
When earth no more shall groan
   Beneath the curse of pain;
But Paradise shall be restored,
   And peace forever reign.

PREFACE.

I OFFER no apology for giving to the community a new book on the sabbath. At a time when there are found so many professing Christianity who coincide with the ungodly in urging forward public measures for the general desecration of that day, it is a duty one owes to God and humanity, to do all he can to preserve from abuse an institution which is the very palladium of heaven's richest blessings of providence and grace. The best way of promoting the observance of any institution, if it be really good, is to disseminate correct views concerning it, presenting it in its true light, showing its Divine appointment, moral nature, absolute necessity, perpetual obligation, and indispensable utility. Common-place as the subject may appear to many, it is intrinsically one of great interest, and by no means exhausted of its attractiveness and force by those who have heretofore written upon it. Beneath the surface of the earth, through which men have driven the plough, and from which they have reaped stores of grain, have laid undiscovered rich mines of precious metal, to reward in the end some diligent laborer, who digging deeper than was wont, shall strike with his spade the hidden vein, and reveal its wealth. The Sabbatical institution has its fertile soil and its rich mines. With earnest desire to find, and diligent application in seeking, I have dug in this field, and now present for the consideration of the reader, and, if found worthy, for his adoption, the thoughts which in this connection have been awakened in my mind. If they are the pure gold of truth, they will stand the test of enlightened Biblical criticism, to which they are cheerfuly submitted. If there be in them any of the base alloy of error, no one will rejoice more in its detection and exposure than I, and no one will be more ready to remove the scum, that the truth may appear in all its Divine and heavenly purity.

I am not aware that any who have written upon the sabbath have taken the view of it here presented. There will be found in this treatise, not only old thoughts in new forms, and some which have perhaps been better expressed by others; but, also, new thoughts now first developed from the germs of Divine truth. The manner in which the subject is treated is also, I believe, entirely new. Yet I have not sought after novelties from any particular penchant for them, but I have sought after truth; and with humble dependence on God, and earnest prayer for the teachings of his Spirit, I have daily searched the Scriptures that I might know the things which are freely given to us of God, joyfully accepting the confirmation, by the testimony of the Word, of those truths which are old; and thankfully receiving, from the same testimony, the knowledge of the truths which are new. And as every scribe instructed unto the kingdom of heaven is likened unto a householder who brings forth out of his treasury things new and old; so, following the order in which they were developed to my understanding, I have, with as much plainness of speech and perspicuity of style as I am master of, endeavored to set forth the truths, whether new or old, respecting the sabbath, and its Lord, which I have found in the treasury of inspiration.

The sabbath is a Divine institution, and belongs legitimately to a Divine religion; for although false religions or corruptions of the true, may have in some instances retained the day, they lost the thing. The weekly division of time, and the observance of the seventh day as a religious festival were retained especially by the Eastern nations after the confusion of tongues and their consequent dispersion from the scene of their folly; but it was to them no longer a real sabbath. Its design, use, and import, were perverted; and, being abused to idolatrous purposes, it was more desecrated in its observance, than it would have been by its neglect. In idolatrous communities the sabbath soon lost its sacredness, and, if observed at all, became a season of the grossest licentiousness and brutality; the restraints of passion were thrown off, and men and women abandoned themselves to every species of vice. The holidays of the heathen were the most unholy of all days, being characterized by an abandonment to sensual dissipation. It is only among the people of God, that, in any age, a sabbath can be found worthy of the name; and among them only as they adhered to the true faith. It is so now also. The more truly evangelical a people are, the more sacredly is the sabbath observed according to the design of the institution. The corruptions of Christianity are characterized by a looseness in regard to the observance of the sabbath. And the more corrupt any Christian community becomes, the more frivolous is the manner of its observance. This is so general, that the manner in which the sabbath is observed among any people, may be taken as a pretty correct index of their religion. A religion without a sabbath would soon fall into desuetude; and a sabbath profaned, neglected, and despised, is an evidence of a corrupt and profligate religion, and the open door for every species of vice and wickedness.

Where the sabbath is observed as it should be, the

people are industrious, prosperous, virtuous, and happy. There true religion holds its sway. There order, peace, and good neighborhood is the rule; and disorder, riot, and crime is the exception. Wickedness dare not lift up its head in the face of a well-kept sabbath. It is therefore the true policy of a government to promote, as far as possible, the due observance of the sabbath. The law of the sabbath, and all other moral laws, are obligatory upon the people in the very nature of things, and by the constitution of their being, as set forth in the commandments of God, independent of the sanction of human laws; but it is the interest of every nation to enforce the observance of morality, and to suppress vice and crime, hence it is their interest to enforce the observance of the sabbath. We should be horrified if the Legislature were to legalize murder, adultery, theft, and perjury. It would be to legislate against the very life and well-being of the community. To legislate against the sabbath is by many regarded as a little thing, and yet it is to legislate against the peace and security of the commonwealth. Any enactment which tends to weaken the obligations of the people to observe the sabbath, or provides for its desecration, weakens, in the same proportion, the power and influence of the civil magistrate, strengthens the bands of the lawless and disobedient, and provides for the increase of licentiousness and every degrading vice. It is easier to keep up and preserve the defenses of virtue and religion than, after they have been broken down for any length of time, to set them up again. The conservators of the public weal would consult the peace and happiness of the people by providing for a more strict observance of the sabbath, instead of breaking down the existing restraints upon its desecration. It is certainly the duty of all Christians who believe that obedience to the Divine laws will ensure the welfare of the people and the tranquillity of the State to use all their influence, legitimately, to prevent any legal authorization of sabbath-breaking, either by individuals or corporations.

To awaken attention to the subject; to furnish information respecting it; to inspire a greater love for it; to induce a more enlightened and conscientious observance of it; and to dissuade others from desecrating the sabbath is the design of my book. And I humbly, yet confidently, submit the views herein presented to all sects and parties for their serious consideration and candid judgment, according to the apostolic injunction, "Prove all things; hold fast that which is good." And as nothing but the truth can make us free from error, and unite us in faith and practice, so I pray that God, by his blessing, may prosper the truth.

Kensington, Philadelphia, 1859.

THE SABBATH AND ITS LORD.

CHAPTER I.

CREATION'S HOLYDAY.

"And he said unto them, The sabbath was made for man, and not man for the sabbath. Therefore the Son of Man is Lord also of the sabbath."—Mark ii. 27, 28.

THE SABBATH IS CREATION'S HOLYDAY, and viewed in relation to its origin, design, adaptations and effects, is a subject of deep interest. It is associated with all that is pure and noble in the creation, history, and destiny of the earth. So essential is it to the well-being of mankind that its due observance is made a moral obligation, sanctioned by the authority of Jehovah himself, when he made Sinai his legislative hall, and from his pavilion of cloud proclaimed the law—"REMEMBER THE SABBATH DAY TO KEEP IT HOLY."

SABBATH is a Hebrew word transferred to our language, and it signifies REST. For in six days God created the heavens and the earth and all their hosts. "And on the seventh day God ended his work which he had made, and he rested on the seventh day from all his work which he had made. And God blessed the seventh day and sanctified it, because that in it he had rested from all his work which God created and made." Gen. ii. 2, 3. How stupendous are the works of God! With wonder and delight we contemplate the production and formation of this magnificent universe. What an immense space is occupied even by the solar system! How grand its central orb of light and heat, its planets, asteroids, moons, and comets! But imagination is overwhelmed and lost in the exceeding vastness of the great unknown beyond, where every twinkling star, the central sun of some vast system, shines.

> "These are thy glorious works, Parent of good,
> Almighty; thine this universal frame,
> Thus wondrous fair; thyself how wondrous then.'

The cosmogony of Moses relates not to the production of matter and the primitive construction of the universe, but to a reconstruction of what is termed the heavens and the earth—referring to this globe and its relations, and the creation of new orders of plants, trees, and animals, and a new race of intelligent beings.

Since the original formation of the universe many changes have no doubt been made in its various parts, as God in his wisdom has seen to be necessary for new modifications of being, or purposes of moral government. The globe on which we dwell has evidently been subject to changes produced by fire and water.

Gen. i. 2—"And the earth was without form and void and darkness was upon the face of the deep, and the Spirit of God moved upon the face of the waters," refers to the state of the earth at the time the Mosaic narrative commences. Of the six days' work, light is said to have been the first creation; but in this passage Moses describes a condition of the earth before light was made, and shows conclusively that the globe on which we dwell existed previous to the creative acts recorded by him. This condition was, in all probability, the result of some great convulsion of nature by which a previous form or condition of it was changed, and the creatures inhabiting it were destroyed. It may have been a general deluge, accompanied with such a change in the atmosphere as rendered it incapable of supporting life or of transmitting light, and so involving all in darkness and death. The geological record indicates that the earth had been inhabited ages before the first human pair was created, and that its pre-Adamic inhabitants were destroyed by some sudden and overwhelming catastrophe. With this the Mosaic narrative agrees, showing that it was without form and void when the six days' work of reorganization and creation began. The six days' work gave to the earth a new condition or form, and furnished it with new trees and plants and new inhabitants. "And God saw every thing that he had made and behold it was very good." And when all were finished he rested on the seventh day. Not that he needed rest: "for the Lord, the Creator of heaven and earth, fainteth not, neither is weary." It did not tire him to create this glorious universe, or reconstruct any part thereof; "for he spake and it was done, he commanded and it stood fast." He found no difficulty and felt no weariness. But it was because the work of reorganization and construction was finished. It was not necessary to keep on creating. All kinds of grass and herbs, and trees yielding fruit, had seed in themselves for reproduction; and all living creatures were formed with power to propagate their species. And when the human pair were fashioned and stood in all the purity and glory of the Divine image, "God blessed them, and God said unto them, Be fruitful and multiply and replenish the earth, and subdue it." Hence new creations were unnecessary. Having made all things perfect in their nature, and suited to the purposes for which they were formed, he rested on the seventh day in a pleasurable contemplation of all his works, which he pronounced "very good."

It was, also, with a view to sanctify to man a day of rest from ordinary occupation and labor, and a season for special devotional service and religious enjoyment. It was not intended that man should be an idler in creation. It was a part of God's plan that he should work. And therefore the Lord God planted a garden eastward in Eden, and there he put the man to dress it and to keep it. There was plenty of pleasant work in the garden, and six days out of every seven were allotted for its performance, and every seventh day was set apart as a sabbath—a day of rest —a period of cessation from delightful labor, for the still more delghtful exercise of praise in the worship of the great Creator of all things. We are not to suppose that the six days' employment of man, in his primitive condition, were wearisome and fatiguing, so as to render the sabbath necessary, in order to recruit his failing energies or refresh his exhausted spirits. It was no drudgery "to prune those growing plants, and tend those flowers," or " to reform the flowery arbors" and "lop the wanton growth" of branches which overhung the "alleys green," their "walk at noon." These labors only gave a richer relish to their food, a healthier tone to the pure blood, and made their sleep at night more sweet. Such labor was adapted to their physical nature, and only tended to preserve the vigor and elasticity of their bodies. It was not to give rest to weary limbs and overtasked muscles; it was not to recruit his wasted strength, and remedy the weekly exhaustion of labor, so as to render him capable of enduring further toil; as if labor were an end, or the products of labor the chief good, that the sabbath was appointed. The institution had not its foundation in any such necessity, or for any such reason. We might argue this from the fact that the first day of man's life was a sabbath. For man was made on the sixth day of creation, and near the close of the day. He was the crowning-piece of the Creator's works and head of all on earth. And the seventh day of creation was the first of man's existence. The sabbath began at the going down of the sun on the sixth day, just after man was made, and placed in the garden: hence the first day of his life was the first sabbath. It did not succeed a week of toil, and was not therefore designed simply to afford him time to recruit his physical strength, for its first observance preceded the labor of the week. The first sabbath found man in all the freshness and glory of his being as he came from the hands of his Creator, and not exhausted and fatigued by previous labor. It was not its great object then to give refreshment to the body.

Nor was the sabbath arbitrarily and capriciously appointed. There existed adequate reasons in the nature of things for the consecration of this portion of time to religious uses. The sabbath was made for man. Even in his primitive state of innocence and purity man needed a sabbath. He was created a religious being—a moral agent, whose duty it was to love and obey his Creator. He was made upright; but his moral character was only to be formed and established by voluntary obedience to the Divine law. He was therefore placed in a state of trial. As a moral agent he could not otherwise attain to an improvement of condition. The circumstances in which he was placed left him free to act according to the volitions of his own mind, with full power to obey the Divine command, that by constancy of obedience he might attain to personal holiness and insure the glory set before him as the end of his trial. Innocent he was made, it could not be otherwise, and endued with power not only to retain his innocency, but through the use of appropriate means to perfect holiness and secure glory higher than creation gave him. In that primitive condition he had duties to perform, ordinances to observe, temptations to endure, and sin to avoid. The great end to be attained was the development, maturity, and perfection of his moral nature. He was not made a mere animal, to eat and drink, to wake and sleep, and otherwise indulge in sensual delights. His intellectual and moral powers stamped him as a being designed for higher and nobler ends. He was made in the image of God, and the object of trial was, that he might, through voluntary obedience, be confirmed in holiness, and so glorify God and enjoy him forever. It was in view of this that the sabbath was instituted. It was to meet the wants of his intellectual and moral nature. It was to be a means of advancing his moral and religious improvement. It was to secure time for more particular attention to divine and heavenly contemplations, and for more intimate communion with God and angels than other days afforded. It was for religious and spiritual exercises. It must, therefore, have had its ordinances of divine worship, in which were commemorated the wisdom, power, and goodness of God as manifested in his glorious works. The sabbath was designed to subserve man's spiritual interests. If he had been made an irrational creature, as the horse or the ox, physical relaxation might have been all that he would have needed, and that might have been sufficiently secured by nightly rest and refreshment in sleep. No sabbath had then been needed. But as man was made a rational being and moral agent, relaxation from labor and business could not satisfy the demands of his nature. Night and sleep give him rest and refreshment for the body. The physical nature is thus satisfied. But he needs something more. The cultivation of his moral and religious nature demands a cessation from toil and business, for a part of his time, that he may attend to spiritual and religious things. The portion of time thus appropriated should be sufficient for the purpose, and made regularly to occur at short intervals. Such is the sabbath day, for which the great Creator saw there would be a necessity in man's moral constitution, and which in his wisdom he graciously set apart for this use. And we may be assured that the amount of time thus devoted to sacred purposes is neither more nor less than man's spiritual need required. And even if no necessity had existed in man's nature for such an ordinance, it would have been proper on account of his relation to and dependence upon God, that a suitable portion of his time should be devoted exclusively to religious uses, and for the expression of his gratitude to the Giver of all good. God is worthy of being honored by a consecration to his worship of a distinct portion of our time, that it may be employed in devout meditation on his nature, perfections, works and ways. But there was a necessity for this ordinance in man's nature; and the exercises of the sabbath day—its religious services—its divine communings were designed to reflect in their action upon man in exalting his mind and promoting his progress in holiness, until he should be completely established in a good character, and prepared for a more exalted condition.

Man was also created a social being, and in this relation was required a community of worship. It was no more good for him to be alone in religious matters than in secular concerns. Congregational worship has its foundation in man's nature. He must in this manner cultivate the social feelings in religion. The religion of an anchoret is unnatural, constrained, and distorted. For social worship it was necessary that there should be a fixed and stated time perpetually recurring. Without this it could not be known when to assemble. It was necessary also that the observance of this portion of time should be vested with all the weight of a moral obligation. Hence the sabbath was sanctified or set apart, by the all-wise Creator and Governor of the universe, as a day of rest or cessation from ordinary labor and secular business and for a religious use. It was not that the day might be spent in idleness; but that it should be appropriated to an active employment in spiritual exercises.

The sabbath was creation's holyday. The works of God were finished when, near or at the close of the sixth day, man was made in the image of his Creator; and the woman, bone of his bone and flesh of his flesh, was given to him as a partner of his life and the sharer of his honors and his joys. Then on the seventh day the Creator rested in a full satisfaction with the works he had made, for they were very good. And he blessed the seventh day. He ordained it to be a blessing to man. It was not for his own use that he blessed it. Every day was alike blessed to him. It was set apart and blessed for man's sake. The sabbath was made for man. The condition of man, though created in knowledge, righteousness, and true holiness, did not place him above the need of it. It was an institution demanded by the nature of man; yea, his condition of trial rendered it highly important if not indispensable. It was sanctified for his use. It was blessed for his benefit. And his very life began with the keeping of the first sabbath as if to remind him of its great design as a religious institution, its importance to the due cultivation of his moral nature, and to endear it to his heart. In man's life and history the sabbath was placed first before all other days, to show that the religious element was the most important, and its culture to be first attended to.

We love to think that the first sabbath, if no more, was observed by our first parents according to its original design. The hypothesis that they sinned and were expelled from the garden of Eden on the very day they were created is not required by any Bible doctrine, and cannot fairly be deduced from the narrative. The contrary appears more consistent. They may have spent many happy days in innocency before the tempter found fit opportunity to ply his temptation and beguile the woman to disobedience. And we love to think that in the blissful bowers of Eden they spent the first day of their lives in celebrating the praise of the glorious Author of the new-made world. It was fit that the holyday of creation should be hallowed by them in the most exalted spiritual intercourse, in divine and heavenly contemplations, in harmonious and delightful praise, and in sublime communion with Jehovah. We love to think that on that day they walked and talked with holy angels, sweetening their intercourse with songs of lofty praise; that they worshiped in the very presence of the Lord God, and learned from him whatever related to their duties as intelligent beings; that then the nature and conditions of the first covenant were made known to them; that the representative character of

Adam—the interests involved—the rewards of obedience and the penalty of transgression, were made known, that they might understand the relations in which they stood, and be armed with every suitable motive to continue in obedience and overcome every temptation to evil.

It was the holyday of creation and the day of their coronation, in which the sovereignty of earth was committed to their hands. They were made a little lower than the angels, they were crowned with glory and honor, they were made to have dominion over the works of God; all things were put under their feet: all sheep and oxen, yea, and the beasts of the field; the fowl of the air, and the fish of the sea, and whatsoever passeth through the paths of the sea. All were made subject to their will. The scene may have excited the envy and malice of the fallen angels; but the holy ones,

> "The morning stars,
> Together sang, and all the sons of God
> Shouted for joy! Loud was the peal: so loud
> As would have quite o'erwhelmed human sense;
> But to the earth it came a gentle strain,
> Like softest fall breathed from Æolian lute,
> When, 'mid the chords, the evening gale expires,
> DAY OF THE LORD! Creation's hallowed close."

CHAPTER II.

REDEMPTION'S WORKING-DAY.

" And he said unto them, The sabbath was made for man, and not man for the sabbath. Therefore the Son of man is Lord also of the Sabbath."—Mark ii. 27, 28.

THE SABBATH IS REDEMPTION'S WORKING-DAY.— Its sanctification to man as a day of rest or cessation from labor and business, did not consign it to indolence or inert repose. Had man not sinned; had he retained his original rectitude and preserved his first estate, the sabbath would still have been occupied actively and delightfully in spiritual and divine exercises. This would have been as necessary for the continuance and improvement of his religious and spiritual life, as the six days' labor would have been to his physical life. Nor is it any less necessary since the fall of man. It is even more necessary. Man's need is greater in every respect. As he needs to labor more and toil harder during the six working days to obtain the meat that perishes; so he needs to improve more assiduously the sabbath day for the advancement of his spiritual life. How long it was after his creation ere man sinned, is a question which belongs not to our present subject. It matters not. God, who foresaw that man would sin, and designed his redemption, determined that the sabbath should be continued to him in his fallen state, associated with such means of grace as would tend to save him from sin and elevate his moral character, and eventually warrant an improvement of his condition. God foresaw that man would need such a day. If he needed it in his primitive state of innocence and happiness, how much more would he need it in his fallen state of sinfulness and misery. And, foreseeing this, the Lord of the Sabbath adapted it to the economy of Redemption; and hence under the regime of salvation the sabbath was made for man, and not man for the sabbath.

It has been a subject of debate among theologians whether the sabbath was given to man as an ordinance prior to the exode of the Israelites from Egypt. It seems evident to my mind that it was divinely instituted with man in his Eden state, and subsequently adapted, as became necessary by the fall of man, to every succeeding dispensation of the economy of grace, according to the Divine will. I shall, therefore, consider it in relation to its aspect before the Law, under the Law, and under the Gospel.

1. THE SABBATH BEFORE THE LAW.

The sabbath was made for man, that is, for mankind; the term man being employed generically for the human race. It was not made for any special class or nation of men. It is not likely that an institution, having its foundation in a necessity of man's nature would be kept secret from him for so long a time as they suppose who maintain that it was first instituted with the Israelites in the wilderness. Adam, in innocence, had his labor assigned to him. His business was to dress the garden of Eden and to keep it. It is unreasonable to suppose that the sabbatical rest was not made known to him; that his Eden state was unblest by any sweet sabbath of communion with God. And when by transgression he involved himself and his posterity in additional toil to overcome the curse which was put upon the ground for man's sake, it is not likely that he would forget the day of rest, or that he would let his posterity forget it. And as the purpose of God to effect the redemption of man from sin and death by the seed of the woman was then revealed, the continuance of the sabbath would not only be a reminiscence of what was lost, but also an antepast of what should be required. In the Antediluvian, as well as in the Postdiluvian times, they had divinely appointed religious institutions; for Abel and Enoch and Noah are commended for their faith. But faith implies a revelation; for faith cometh by hearing, and hearing by the word of God. There were doubtless revelations made adapted to the wants of the age; and revelations have usually been associated with religious institutions, such as sacrifices and offerings, and these have uniformly been associated with appointed times for their performance. Now the sabbath has always been the principal time for the offering of sacrifices and special attention to religious duties. In Gen. iv. 3, 4, it is written that, " in process of time," or as it is literally, "at the end of days," "it came to pass that Cain brought of the fruit of the ground an offering to the Lord. And Abel also brought of the firstlings of his flock and of the fat thereof." At the end of days refers to some well-known division and termination of days. The week is the only division of days mentioned by Moses in his history of that early age, and there is no time so likely to be designated as the end of days as the seventh day or sabbath, coming as it did at the termination of the week, and no other upon which, by common agreement, they would be likely to offer their sacrifices and perform their devotions. It was the day set apart for such services; and it is a legitimate inference that they observed the sabbath, bringing on that day their offerings to the Lord to the place which he had designated for their public worship to be paid.

The weekly division of time is referred to in Gen. vii. 4, where it is written "For yet *seven days* and I will cause it to rain on the earth." We suppose that Noah, to whom this was said, was in the habit of offering his sacrifices unto the Lord at the appointed place of worship on the sabbath day; and that the Lord God met with him there, and, on the occasion referred to, revealed to him, that after the expiration of another week, *seven days*, the deluge should begin. So also in Gen. viii. 10, 12, we find that Noah having sent forth a dove to ascertain whether the waters were abated, and it having returned to him without any evidence of it, waited "yet *other seven days*," and sent it forth again, when it returned in the evening with an olive leaf in its mouth. And again he waited "yet *other seven days*" and sent it forth again. Thus we find him acting in regard to the regular weekly division to time. And as this weekly division of time had its origin in the six days of creation and one of rest, it is rendered certain

3*

that the institution, nature, and design of the sabbath was known to Noah, it having been observed from the creation of the world, by the family of Seth.

Again, there is reference made to this weekly division of time in the institution of the Passover, when the Lord brought the children of Israel out of Egypt. "Seven days," said he, "thou shalt eat unleavened bread, and in the seventh day shall be a feast to the Lord." Ex. xiii. 6. They were to eat unleavened bread for a week, and the seventh day of the week was to be the festival of the sabbath, which is pre-eminently called the Lord's festival, the day on which he rested from his works and was refreshed.

Thus it appears to have been usual for God's people in the ages before the law to observe the weekly division of time. And we may justly conclude that the Sabbath was known to, and observed by them from the creation down to the exode of the Israelites from Egypt. Manassah-ben-Israel, a Jewish doctor, says, that "according to the tradition of the ancients, Abraham and his posterity, having preserved the memory of the creation, observed the sabbath also, in consequence of the natural law to that purpose." Philo, another Jewish writer, says, "that the sabbath is not a festival peculiar to any one people or country, but is common to the whole world; and that it may be named the general or public festival, and that of the nativity of the world."

Finally, it appears from the narrative in Exodus xvi., that the sabbath had been known and observed before the giving of the law. The seed of Abraham have been from the beginning a chosen and peculiar people, designed, in the economy of redemption, for a special purpose, and to that end subjected to a course of physical, political, and moral training, differing from other nations, and best adapted to secure the object in view. Their deliverance from Egyptian bondage by a series of stupendous miracles, by which the magicians of Egypt were confounded, and the pride of her kings and princes was brought low, was designed to make known to them the power and majesty of the great I AM, awaken toward him their reverential fear, encourage their loving confidence, and impress their minds with a conviction of the folly and wickedness of idolatry. And they were led into the trials of the wilderness to test their faith in God, convince them of their entire dependence upon him, and develop a due sense of their obligations to obey him; to humble them, and prove them; to know what was in their heart, and whether they would keep his commandments or no. Take for instance the miraculous supply of food; for he suffered them to hunger, and then fed them with manna, that he might make them understand that man doth not live by bread alone; but by every word that proceedeth out of the mouth of the Lord doth man live. Scarcely had they passed through the Red Sea, and reached the desert bordering upon its eastern shore, before their provision failed and they began to murmur, and complained that they had been brought from a land of plenty into an inhospitable wilderness, to perish by famine. Then the Lord shamed their murmurings by the gift of manna, which, in the night, fell round about their camp and afforded them an abundant supply of nutritious and wholesome food; as it is written, "He gave them bread from heaven and man did eat angels' food." The manna was a small round thing—small as the hoar frost, and it lay on the ground after the dew was gone up. And Moses said to the people, "This is the bread which the Lord hath given you to eat." And they gathered as much of it as they needed for the day, every man according to the number of persons in his tent. It was like coriander seed, white; and the taste of it was like wafers made with honey. It was their daily bread, and none of it was to be left until the next day; for if kept over night, it bred worms and became offensive to the smell. But when the sixth day came, the people generally gathered double the usual quantity, so as to have enough for the seventh day, which was the sabbath. This they did, notwithstanding the manna had always corrupted after the first day if any was left over until the morrow. This they did without any special instructions from the Lord concerning it, evidently from a habit of providing on the sixth day for the necessities of the seventh, that they might observe it as a day of rest, and divining that he who gave the manna for their food would also preserve it from corrupting on the seventh day, that they might not violate the sabbath by having to gather it on that day. And the rulers of the people who superintended the business went and told Moses, that they might ascertain whether it were right for the people to do this. And Moses having presented the case before the Lord, was told to answer them as follows: "To-morrow is the rest of the holy sabbath unto the Lord: bake that which you will bake to-day, and seethe that which you will seethe; and that which remaineth over lay up for you to be kept until the morning." And they did so, and it corrupted not; and Moses told them to eat that on the sabbath, for they should not find any in the field. But some of the people having neglected to gather on the sixth day for the seventh, either because they did not sufficiently regard the sabbath, or because they supposed that the manna would spoil as usual, and be unfit for food even if they did gather it, went out on the sabbath morning into the field to gather it, but they found none. And God said to Moses, "How long refuse ye to keep my commandments and my laws. See, for that the Lord hath given you the sabbath, therefore he giveth you, on the sixth day, the bread of two days: abide ye every man in his place; let no man go out of his place on the seventh day. So the people rested on the seventh day."

Now these things occurred some time before the giving of the Law from Sinai; and they show that the seventh day of the week had been known and observed as a divinely-instituted sabbath before the promulgation of the Decalogue and the special national laws were enacted by the Holy One of Israel. The narrative shows, that the people generally on this occasion, and under peculiar circumstances tending rather to deter them from it, made provision for the due observance of the seventh day as a time of cessation from all labor and secular business. The manna must have begun to fall upon the first day of the week, after Moses had presented the necessities of the people before the Lord on the preceding sabbath. It fell for six consecutive days, and would not keep so as to be fit to eat on the next day after it fell. It had to be gathered fresh every morning. And yet on the sixth day the people, without any instruction in relation thereto, proceeded to gather double quantity on the sixth day. They probably saw that the supply that had fallen was double as much as on any other day, and inferred from this circumstance that it was designed to furnish them with food for the sabbath day. This was before the giving of the Law. The conduct of the people was approved by the Lord, as it evidently was founded upon their regard for his ordinances and their faith in his providence. He therefore declared that it was in accordance with his will concerning the sabbath, which being commemorative of his resting from his works of creation was a holyday unto him. Those who neglected to make this provision for the sabbath, and went out to gather manna on the seventh day, were severely rebuked for their impiety, which is spoken of as one of a long series of similar transgressions of commandments and laws already existing and known to them. The laws and commandments here referred to, and by which the sabbath was given to them, must have been such as had been from the beginning, and which were known and handed down from generation to generation. It follows then that the sabbath had been previously known to them as a Divine Institution. It was an ordinance of the Lord, which his people had all along been accustomed to observe. It is not spoken of as an institution then first enjoined upon them, but as one that had always been in force from the creation of the world. But the circumstances in connection with the giving of the manna were calculated to induce a greater regard for the sabbath, since so wonderful a provision was made for its observance. It was calculated to impress upon their minds the sacredness in which the God of Israel regarded the sabbath, and to prepare them for the special enactment concerning its observance under the Law.

We may certainly conclude, then, that the sabbath had been strictly observed in the times before the law; that Abel and Enoch and Noah, and all the people of God of the antediluvian age, observed it and kept it holy unto the Lord. That subsequently Noah and Shem, and Abraham and his seed, pepetuated its remembrance and delighted in its holy and sanctifying services.

> " Yes! blessed sabbath morn, thy light
> Is affluent of pure delight
>   To those who love thy rest ;
> Beyond thy sun, a heavenly ray
> Adds moral lustre to the day,
>   And shines into the breast."

2. THE SABBATH UNDER THE LAW.

As the sabbath was made for man, so it became man's duty to observe the sabbath. The reasons for the institution exist, as I have previously shown, in man's nature and relations, and give it the force of a moral obligation. It is absolutely necessary for man's good, necessary to the proper development of his religious and spiritual nature; necessary to the maturity and establishment of his moral character. It has, hence, been placed among man's moral duties. The Decalogue, or ten commandments promulged from Sinai, was not then an act of new legislation. It was merely the formal utterance of principles which had existed as moral laws in the nature and relations of mankind from the beginning. They had always existed, though man's depravity and ignorance had obscured his perception of them, and had almost obliterated them from his mind. In the line of the patriarchs and their adherents these principles were known, being revived in their minds from time to time by Divine interposition and revelation. And when the Lord came down upon mount Sinai, in the sight of all the people of Israel, to give them his statutes and ordinances, and to separate them unto himself as a peculiar people above all the nations of the earth, he proclaimed the moral law as the basis or foundation of the entire civil and religious code which he was about to give them through the ministration of his servant Moses. The proclamation of the law was attended with the most impressive circumstances. For three days the people sanctified themselves; and on the third day in the morning there were thunders and lightnings, and a thick cloud upon the mount, and the voice of the trumpet exceeding loud, so that all the people trembled. And Mount Sinai was altogether on a smoke, because the Lord descended upon it in fire, and the smoke thereof ascended as the smoke of a furnace, and the whole mount quaked greatly. And when the voice of the trumpet sounded long and waxed louder and louder, Moses spake and God answered him by a voice. And God spake these words as the fourth commandment of the Decalogue, "REMEMBER THE SABBATH DAY TO KEEP IT HOLY. Six days shalt thou labor and do all thy work; but the seventh is the sabbath of the Lord thy God; in it thou shalt not do any work, thou, nor thy son, nor thy daughter, nor thy man servant, nor thy maid servant, nor thy cattle, nor thy stranger that is within thy gates; for in six days the Lord made heaven and earth, the sea and all that in them is, and rested the seventh day. Wherefore the Lord blessed the seventh day and hallowed it."

Now observe that this command is incorporated with all other moral commands, and is therefore one of them, and they were all written by the finger of God upon tables of stone, to indicate their perpetual obligation. But these moral precepts, given in this formal manner to the Israelites only, were not binding on them exclusively; they are obligatory upon all mankind. All intelligent creatures, when placed in relations contemplated by the law, are bound to obey the law. It is obligatory upon all men to worship God and him only—to avoid idolatry and profanity, and equally so to remember the sabbath day to keep it holy. Cessation from worldly business and labor for the meat that perisheth, devotion to religious services in the worship of God, and the culture of the spiritual and moral powers and affections, are no less necessary to other men than to the Jew. All needed the sabbath, and the sabbath had from the beginning been given to all. But to meet an exigency which God foresaw would arise through the general defection of mankind from his worship and their prostitution to idolatry; to provide a national depository for the oracles of truth; to preserve the true religion from utter extinction, and to carry on by the best instrumentality the great work of redemption, God saw fit to call Abraham, and to separate his seed to himself as a peculiar people. In the promise made to him and his seed of the land of Canaan for an everlasting inheritance, and that in him and in his seed should all the families of the earth be blessed, was included the kingdom of heaven which God purposes to establish upon the earth, and of which the seed of Abraham are to be the heirs. The covenant thus made regarded primarily the seed of faith, who, begotten by the word of truth, are the children of promise, and shall be made kings and priests in that kindom. It also had respect to the natural seed, in whom it was to be tested whether it were practicable or not to prepare a nation in natural flesh for such a glorious destiny. When therefore God essayed to go and take them "from the midst of another nation, by temptations, by signs, and by wonders, and by war, and by a mighty hand, and by a stretched out arm, and by great terrors," as he did in Egypt, it was to make himself known to them as the only living and true God, to instruct them and train them up for the inheritance, the everlasting possession of which was promised to them nationally on condition that they should obey his voice and keep the statutes and commandments which he gave them. Hence to them in this relation pertained "the adoption, and the glory, and the covenants, and the giving of the law, and the service of God, and the promises."

These belonged to them nationally as long as their national trial lasted, and to no other nation. These belonged to them not absolutely but conditionally; and God separated them as a nation to himself, and nourished and instructed them in the wilderness, and planted them in the land of Canaan under laws and institutions, which if obeyed, would have insured to them the fulfillment of the promises and the possession of the glory.

Among the ordinances which he gave them, the observance of the sabbath in its connection with the worship of God, and because of its moral and saving influence upon the hearts and the minds of the people, was made pre-eminent. Its observance was strictly enjoined upon them by special enactment and enforced by severe penalties. Thus God said, "Verily my sabbath ye shall keep; for it is a sign between me and you, throughout your generations, that ye may know that I am the Lord that doth sanctify you. Ye shall keep the sabbath therefore; for it is holy unto you: every one that defileth it shall surely be put to death; for whosoever doth any work therein, that soul shall be cut off from among his people: Six days may work be done: but in the seventh is the Sabbath of rest, holy to the Lord, whosoever doth any work in the sabbath day, he shall surely be put to death. Wherefore the children of Israel shall keep the sabbath, to observe the sabbath throughout their generations, for a perpetual covenant. It is a sign between me and the children of Israel forever: for in six days the Lord made heaven and earth and on the seventh day he rested and was refreshed." Ex. xxxi. 13–17. We can scarcely estimate the importance here attached to the observance of the sabbath by the nation of Israel. We may approximate thereto by a consideration of the nature and end of the sabbath as the sign of their national covenant. The end to be attained by the nation through a truly religious and devout observance of the sabbath was their national sanctification in the flesh and consequent possession of the glory and blessedness of the kingdom of God. It was to be the means of attaining the highest degree of spiritual life and the highest condition of dignity and happiness. It was therefore a crime of great turpitude to defile that holy day; for it was to aim a deadly blow at the eternal life, blessedness and glory of the nation. The nation of Israel were, by the terms of the covenant God made with them, in a state of trial similar to that of Adam in the Garden of Eden. The covenant with Adam involved the life of all his seed to be perpetually prolonged by access to the tree of life on condition of his obedience; but the penalty of his transgression was death to all: and the tree of the knowledge of good and evil was the sign through which his obedience was tested. So in God's covenant with Israel the sabbath was chosen as the sign through which their obedience was tested. An unbroken observance of the sabbath by the nation would have secured to them the everlasting possession of the kingdom and its glory; but for its national profanation they were to be cut off therefrom. Individual defection, if visited according to the command of God with the penalty of death by the national authority, would not vitiate the covenant. But if in their national capacity they failed to execute the penalty from fear of or favor to the criminal, then the sin became national, and the covenant was broken. An instance illustrative of this is given in the case of the man who was found gathering sticks upon the sabbath day. And they that found him gathering sticks, brought him to Moses and Aaron and all the congregation; and they put him in ward, because it was not declared what should be done unto him. The special enactment before quoted had indeed declared that whosoever defiled the sabbath should be put to death, that whosoever did any work therein should be cut off from among his people; but it had not been declared in what manner he should be executed. It was therefore referred to the Lord, and the answer to Moses was, "The man shall surely be put to death; all the congregation shall stone him with stones without the camp." It was to be the act of all the congregation. The crime he had committed was against the whole nation, and the nation were by their act to put away the evil from among them and free themselves from the guilt of polluting the sabbath. The national interests required it—the everlasting well-being of the whole congregation required that this, as well as other violations of the covenant by individuals, should be punished with death. And a failure to execute the penalty would involve the nation in the guilt, and cause them to be cut off from the blessings of the covenant.

The covenant God made with them as recorded in Ex. xix. 5, 6, "Now, therefore, if ye will obey my voice indeed, and keep my covenant, then ye shall be a peculiar treasure unto me above all people: for all the earth is mine: and ye shall be unto me a kingdom of priests and a holy nation," extended throughout all their generations from the exode until the coming of the Messiah in the flesh to confirm the same; but it was made or renewed with each generation on condition of their obeying his voice and keeping his covenant. But this they did not do: for God testifies against them by his prophet Ezekiel, that when he chose Israel in the land of Egypt and promised to be their God, and lifted up his hand to bring them forth out of Egypt into a land flowing with milk and honey, he said to them, "Cast ye away every man the abomination of his eyes, and defile not yourselves with the idols of Egypt." But they rebelled against him and would not hearken: yet he brought them into the wilderness and gave them statutes and showed them judgments, which if a man do he shall even live in them, that is, their life should be perpetually secured by their obedience; and gave them his sabbaths to be a sign between him and them, in which their obedience should be tested, that they might know (prove) that he was the Lord that sanctified them. But the whole house of Israel rebelled against him in the wilderness, walked not in his statutes, despised his judgments, and polluted his sabbaths; so that generation was cut off, and the covenant was renewed with their children, whom he brought into the promised land, and to whom he said, "Walk not in the ways of your fathers, but walk in my statutes and keep my judgments and do them; and hallow my sabbaths; and they shall be a sign between me and you, that ye may know that I am the Lord your God." But they likewise rebelled and obeyed not the voice of the Lord, and polluted his sabbaths, and so generation after generation broke the covenant and were cut off, until at last the trial of the natural seed ended, and they have since been scattered among the nations, and dispersed through the countries, as in lifting up his hand he declared they should be, because they executed not his jugments and despired his statutes, and polluted his sabbaths, and their eyes were after their idols. Ezek. xx. 2-24.

Promises of national honor, glory, and blessedness were repeatedly made to them throughout their generations, and in such terms as accord with the original covenant. Of this we have several instances recorded in the prophets. Thus in Isaiah lviii. 13, 14, after admonishing them to obey the statutes of the Lord, and promising a great reward corresponding to their faithfulness, he says, "If thou turn away thy foot from the sabbath, from doing thy pleasure on my holy day; and call the sabbath a delight, the holy of the Lord, honorable; and shalt honor him, not doing thine own ways, nor finding thine own pleasure, nor speaking thine own words; then shalt thou delight thyself in the Lord; and I will cause thee to ride upon the high places of the earth, and feed thee with the heritage of Jacob thy father; for the mouth of the Lord hath spoken it." Here we have the renewal of the covenant to that generation in the promise of all its special blessings on condition that they would obey his voice and keep his sabbaths. If obedient, they were to possess the high places of the earth—the supreme government of all nations, and enjoy the heritage of Jacob their father, embracing all the blessings of the covenant God had made with Abraham, and therefore the kingdom and greatness of the kingdom under the whole heaven. Again it is written, Jeremiah xvii. 24, 25, "And it shall come to pass, if ye diligently hearken to me, saith the Lord, to bring in no burden through the gates of this city on the sabbath day, but hallow the sabbath day to do no work therein; then shall there enter into the gates of this city kings and princes sitting upon the throne of David, riding in chariots and on horses, they and their princes, the men of Judah and the inhabitants of Jerusalem together: and this city shall remain forever." In this place the covenant is again renewed with another generation with the promise of making them kings and princes in an everlasting polity on condition of their obedience. And had they kept the covenant, then the tabernacle of David had never fallen, and the kingdom of heaven would have been confirmed and established in their hands. Once more, in Psalm lxxxi. 13–16, God says, "O that my people had hearkened unto me, and Israel had walked in my ways! I should soon have subdued their enemies, and turned my hand against their adversaries. The haters of the Lord should have submitted themselves unto him; but their time should have endured forever. He would have fed them also with the finest of wheat, and with honey out of the rock should I have satisfied thee." Here we find that if they had fulfilled the conditions of the covenant, their enemies should have been subdued to their sway, the haters of the Lord should have been subjected and reconciled to his government through their instrumentality, and their time should have endured forever in the enjoyment of the richest blessings of grace and providence. And when at last the Messiah came, and the hills and vales of Judea resounded with the voice of one crying in the wilderness, "Prepare ye the way of the Lord, make his paths straight," a final offer of the kingdom of heaven was made to the nation in the generation then living on condition of their repentance and bringing forth the fruits suitable thereto. But they knew not the time of their gracious visitation. They turned not from the iniquity of their doings, and their sin reached its culmination in their willful and malicious rejection of the Messiah. Hence Jesus exclaimed, "O Jerusalem, Jerusalem, thou that killest the prophets and stonest them that are sent unto thee! how often would I have gathered thy children together even as a hen gathereth her chickens under her wings, and ye would not! Behold, your house is left unto you desolate. For I say unto you, Ye shall not see me henceforth, till ye shall say, Blessed is he that cometh in the name of the Lord." Matthew xxiii. 37–39. "How often would I have gathered thy children together," refers to his reiterated offers of the salvation and glory of the kingdom to all their generations from the time in which he brought them out of Egypt until that moment in which he contemplated the desolation of their city and temple, and their long dispersion and tribulation. For he it was who was with them in the wilderness and went before them in the pillar of cloud and the pillar of fire; who gave them his laws and statutes from Mount Sinai, and appointed the sabbath as the sign of their obedience. He it was who brought them into the promised land and established his tabernacle among them, and sent them his prophets, rising up early and sending them. And he it was who, having become incarnate, wept over their continued disobedience and their consequent desolation and misery. Previous generations had broken the covenant, and the Divine judgments had fallen upon them; but those judgments were not final, because the time of trial had to be prolonged from one generation to another until the Messiah should come. But when Christ had come and they had consummated their national unbelief and disobedience by rejecting and crucifying him, the wrath came upon them to the uttermost, and they were cut off and dispersed among the nations, until at the time of the second advent of Christ, they shall be restored, and shall, on beholding him coming in the glory of his Father, say, "Blessed is he that cometh in the name of the Lord."

We see, then, in connection with their national covenant and trial, how important the sabbath was to them, being made the sign and test of their obedience. Nehemiah, when he was governor of Judea, says, "In those days saw I in Judah some treading winepresses on the sabbath, and bringing in sheaves, and lading asses; as also wine, grapes, and figs and all manner of burdens which they brought into Jerusalem on the sabbath day. And I testified against them in the day wherein they sold victuals. There dwelt men of Tyre also therein which brought fish, and all manner of ware, and sold on the sabbath unto the children of Judah and in Jerusalem. Then I contended with the nobles of Judah, and said unto them, What evil is this that ye do, and profane the sabbath day? Did not your fathers thus, and did not our God bring all this evil upon us and upon this city? yet ye bring more wrath upon Israel by profaning the sabbath." Neh. xiii. 15-18. It was this national desecration of the sabbath which, from generation to generation, brought upon them the wrath of God. Not that this was their only sin, or even their chief sin; for other and greater sins are charged against them; but the sabbath having been selected as a sign or test, its proper sanctification would have been proof of their obedience in other matters also; and its desecration was a manifest evidence of their rebellion and wickedness. When they profaned the sabbath, it was a proof that they obeyed not the voice of the Lord and kept not his covenant. Hence the Lord said, "If ye will not hearken unto me to hallow the sabbath, and not to bear a burden, even entering in at the gates of Jerusalem on the sabbath day; then will I kindle a fire in the gates thereof, and it shall devour the palaces of Jerusalem, and it shall not be quenched." Jeremiah xvii. 27. And so at last when their trial terminated as already shown, the Jewish nationality was totally subverted, and their city and country have ever since been trodden down of the gentiles: the fire has devoured their palaces and they are a dispersed and afflicted people.

But as their national covenant could not be vitiated by the sin or transgressions of individuals as long as they executed the judgments of God against such; so the blessings of the covenant were not forfeited to those who believed in and obeyed God by the national infidelity: "For what if some did not believe, shall their unbelief make the faith of God without effect? By no means." God is true to his covenant of grace, and faithful to his promise in Christ. And in all generations there has been a remnant who by faith have been justified before God, and to whom the fulfillment of the promise is pledged. Hence the Lord said, "Keep ye judgment and do justice; for my salvation is near to come, and my righteousness to be revealed. Blessed is the man that doth this, and the son of man that layeth hold upon it, that keepeth the sabbath from polluting it, and keepeth his hand from doing any evil. Nether let the son of the stranger that hath joined himself to the Lord speak, saying, The Lord hath utterly separated me from his people; neither let the eunuch say, Behold, I am a dry tree. For thus saith the Lord unto the eunuchs that keep my sabbaths, and choose the things that please me, and take hold of my covenant; even unto them will I give in my house, and within my walls, a place and a name better than of sons and daughters. I will give them an everlasting name that shall not be cut off. Also the sons of the strangers that join themselves unto the Lord, to serve him, and to love the name of the Lord, to be his servants, every one that keepeth the sabbath from polluting it, and taketh hold of my covenant; even them will I bring to my holy mountain, and make them joyful in my house of prayer." Isa. lvi. 1-7. Thus we learn that notwithstanding God foresaw that the result of the national trial of the natural seed would terminate in their rejection in consequence of their continued violation of the covenant throughout their generations, still their unbelief as a nation has not rendered void the promise of God in relation to individuals; but provision was made in accordance with foreknowledge for the salvation of all who believed in God's word; not only of the natural seed, but also of strangers—others than Israelites—who became sincere proselytes, and joined themselves to the Lord, kept the sabbath, and took hold of the covenant. And with this agrees the saying, "Though Israel be as the sand of the sea, yet a remnant shall be saved."

The sabbath is Redemption's working-day, and divinely appointed to be such to the Jewish people nationally and individually. By a strict obedience to the Lord's commands, in walking in his statutes and ordinances, executing his judgments and hallowing his sabbaths, it was in their power as a nation to have obtained the kingdom, to have been made a peculiar people unto the Lord above all the nations of the earth, to have been made a kingdom of priests and a holy nation. That was the prize set before them and promised to them on their fulfillment of the terms of the covenant. "But their heart was not right with him, neither were they steadfast in his covenant." Instead therefore of working out their national redemption, they brought upon themselves the curses written in the book, and were finally excluded from the blessings of the covenant. Their rejection was their own fault, as is seen in the fact that some of Israel have in every generation through faith taken hold of the covenant and have received the promise of eternal life. And what some have done, all might have done. The sabbath and the moral influences associated therewith have not been employed in vain by any one desirous of working out his salvation before God; for through those instrumentalities God wrought in them to will and to do of his good pleasure.

The first and most important point in regard to the sabbath was to sanctify it. "Remember the sabbath day to keep it holy." This command related to its use as a day of special religious services. On this day the priests sacrificed two lambs for a burnt-offering, with wine and meal, and placed on the golden table twelve new loaves of show-bread in place of the stale ones, which were then removed. These loaves represented the twelve tribes, who could not all appear personally in the temple, but who kept the sabbath in their places of abode or dwellings. And the bread was called the bread of faces or bread of the presence, because, representing the twelve tribes, it was designed to indicate their appearing in the presence of the Lord every sabbath day. And the pious Jew knew that, as he worshiped in a distant part of the land with his face toward the temple, he was thus represented by the fresh cakes on the golden table every sabbath and through the whole week. Every tribe and every individual belonging to the tribe was embraced in this representation, and every one knew the hours appointed for sacrifice and prayer, and could join in the worship wherever he might be; for he who dwelt between the cherubim, was everywhere present to accept the offerings of the sincere worshiper. "The eyes of the Lord are in every place, beholding the evil and the good." The sabbath was further appropriately spent in doing good works; in prayer, thanksgiving and praise; in the study of the law of God, and in devout and heavenly contemplations of his nature, character, perfections and purposes.

The next point was that it should be strictly kept as a day of rest from all secular employment. It was not lawful for any one to pursue his business or trade on that day. Every occupation of a worldly character was prohibited. It was not even allowed to kindle a fire for the purpose of cooking or performing any menial or servile labor. The man-servant and maid-servant were to rest as well as their master, and every preparation to that end was to be made on the previous day, which was therefore called the day of preparation. Works of necessity and mercy only were allowed. They might feed and water their cattle, or if any of their animals fell into a pit, they might lift it out. Jesus, who understood the true nature and extent of the law, and who did always those things which were acceptable to God, performed works of benevolence, such as healing the sick and curing the lame and the blind; and laid down the maxim in opposition to the superstition of the Pharisees, that it was lawful to do good on the sabbath days.

Now, though the nation was delinquent in enforcing as it should the law of the sabbath, and broke the covenant, forfeiting all right to the distinguished blessings promised to them as a nation; yet such persons as remembered the sabbath in this manner, abstaining from all work or secular employment, and employing its sacred hours in the service of God and humanity, found that the sabbath was pre-eminently conducive to their sanctification and the promotion of their religious and spiritual advancement. They thus attained to the end of its institution, and their faith took hold of the promised rest which remaineth to the people of God. They all, indeed, died in faith, not having received the promises, but having seen them afar off, were persuaded of them and embraced them. They looked for their fulfillment at the time of the better resurrection which they anticipated, as secured by the promise itself to all who being the seed of faith shall be blessed with faithful Abraham. The sabbath was a sign between them and God, and it shed upon them the sanctifying influences of a glorious hope, which nerved their souls with strength in trial, armed them with patience in suffering, made them more than conquerors over the world, and cheered them in their last moments.

But it had this effect only upon those who had faith in the promises, and whose obedience was the offspring of faith. A mere formal, legal, and hypocritical observance of that day produced no such effect. And such an observance of the day was not acceptable to God. All religious services to be accepted of him must be sincere. He says in Isa. i. 13, "Bring no more vain oblations—incense is an abomination unto me—the new moons and sabbaths and the calling of assemblies I cannot away with." God did not ordain these things merely for the sake of them, or because he had any pleasure in them; but he ordained them as modes of giving expression to faith, and as means of sincere and true worship. When offered in faith; when attended to with a devout and sincere mind, they had a pleasing savor; but otherwise they were an abomination;

> "For God abhors the sacrifice
> Where not the heart is found."

In the time of our Saviour the scribes and Pharisees were very strict in their legal observance of the sabbath as a day of cessation from labor, as well as punctillious in their attention to other rites and ceremonies; but their religion was all an outside show, a little gilding over the surface while all within was rotten. There was no faith at bottom; there was no spirituality in their religion. It was merely a form and possessed no life-giving power. Their religion was a mere cloak with which they sought to conceal their robbery, extortion and uncleanness. But they who sanctified the sabbath according to the Divine command, were sanctified in turn by its reflex influence upon their minds and hearts. They were elevated to a higher and holier atmosphere of love and duty. They had communion and fellowship with God, and found the sabbath a delight, in which they seemed to taste of the powers of the world to come.

> "The All-beneficent
> Cares for man's better nature, and has given
> The sabbath-rest to lead his thoughts to heaven.

> Myriads of thanks for this divinest gift,
> For this perpetually recurring day—
>   Wherein both rich and poor—bond—free—can lift
> Their hopes above this fading world, and pray."
>
>   R. J. EAMES.

3. THE SABBATH UNDER THE GOSPEL.

The sabbath is redemption's working-day. It was originally set apart for man's use and benefit, as necessary for the proper development of his religious and moral nature, even in a state of innocence. It became still a greater necessity after his fall into sin, inasmuch as his condition then presented greater obstructions to the culture of his inward and spiritual life. Man had to be redeemed from sin, and in the work of redemption, the sabbath could not be dispensed with. I have shown that it must have been known and observed before the giving of the Law on Mount Sinai. Eusebius says, "Almost all the philosophers and poets acknowledge the seventh day as holy." And Philo says, "The seventh day is a festival to every nation." And when the Lord separated unto himself the children of Israel, the seed of Abraham his friend, for a special purpose, he constituted the sabbath as a sign between himself and them, a test of their obedience in relation to the covenant he made with them when he took them by the hand to bring them out of Egypt. But the children of Israel did not keep the sabbath. Generation after generation broke the covenant, and thus was demonstrated the impracticability of sanctifying a nation in natural flesh, for the glory and blessedness of the kingdom. The law, including not only the moral precepts of the decalogue, but also the whole civil and ecclesiastical code of Israel, was given as the only means whereby they could nationally be sanctified and prepared for the commitment to them of the Divine government over the world. Obedience to the law was the only ground of justification nationally. The result of their trial showed that by the deeds of the law shall no flesh living be justified in the sight of God. The seed of Abraham was as good a seed and as well, if not better, adapted for such a trial as any that fallen humanity could furnish. Indeed, their election of God for the purpose of trial is sufficient evidence that there were none better. It was not necessary, therefore, on their failure, to make trial of any other nation in like manner. The result would have been the same. A mason wishing stone of a particular quality chooses the best he can find in the quarry, and if it stand not the test, he does not deem it necessary to try every stone separately, but rejects the whole; so God having tried one nation of men in natural flesh, has in them tested and rejected all nations. The trial of any other would only have furnished additional evidence of the fact that "flesh and blood," or men in natural flesh, "cannot inherit the kingdom of God." None can be qualified in natural flesh to be kings and priests in that kingdom. This is the great truth demonstrated by the trial of the natural seed of Abraham. This was foreseen by the Omniscient One, and provision was made for the justification, sanctification, and final salvation of a righteous seed on entirely different grounds. For what the law could not do in that it was weak or inefficient through the flesh; not weak in itself—the provisions of the law were adequate to the end proposed—but weak on account of human depravity and corruption; what, through this weakness, the law could not do, God otherwise accomplished through the gift of his Son, whom he sent to be the propitiation for our sins, that by faith in him we might be justified from all things from which we could not be justified by the deeds of the law. The foundation for justification on this plan was laid in the revelation of the Divine purpose by the declaration that the seed of the woman should bruise the serpent's head, and also by the promise to Abraham, that in him and in his seed should all the families of the earth be blessed. Thus the Gospel was before the law, and from Abel down to Moses there was a seed of faith; believers in the promise being counted for the seed. And after the giving of the law, while the Jewish nation were tried as to their ability to justify themselves by the deeds of the law, individuals of the nation, believing in the promise, were justified by faith. For the law which was added for the trial of the natural seed was not against the promise of God; but only more clearly demonstrated the necessity of the promise, and served as a schoolmaster to bring them to Christ. The plan of justification by faith was not rendered imperative by the law. It continued in force, and by it a remnant of Israel was saved, and constituted a chosen, sanctified and peculiar company. Israel were not all saved, though all might have been saved by faith. Their failure to attain the qualifications necessary to inherit the kingdom in natural flesh, was no bar to their becoming heirs thereof in spiritual and glorified bodies through faith. Those who did believe were made heirs, and all might have believed; but they, ignorant of God's righteousness—of his plan of justifying the ungodly—went about to establish their own righteousness—seeking justification by the deeds of the law—not submitting themselves to the righteousness of God. Hence they were broken off, through or on account of unbelief. Their unbelief left them powerless against the corruption of their own hearts. Their unbelief shut them up in the darkness of their own minds. Their unbelief made the word of God of no effect unto them; so that it did them no good, not being mixed with faith in them that heard it. Their unbelief made their table a snare and a stumbling block unto them, and the provision intended for their good became their overthrow—the occasion of their condemnation. And thus their national trial ended in their rejection as a nation, and rendered necessary a change of dispensation. Many of the natural branches had been broken off because of unbelief, and God determined to graft in upon the stock as many of the gentiles as should believe the Gospel, to supply their place in the coming kingdom. Hence the Gospel dispensation was instituted to take out of the gentiles a people for his name, who, together with the saved of Israel, shall at last be made a royal priesthood, a holy nation, a peculiar people, to whom the administration of the kingdom may in wisdom and righteousness be committed. Hence the Gospel is preached for the obedience of the faith among all nations. And whosoever believeth becomes identified with Christ, is grafted into the good olive tree, is one of Abraham's seed, and an heir according to the promise. Under this new regime, the sabbath is still Redemption's working-day. The fourth commandment has not been abrogated. The sabbath is still to be observed. Its use as a day of cessation from labor and business, and appropriation to our religious and moral culture, is as much needed as ever. But the sabbath is not now a sign to us, as it was to the Jew during the time of his national trial; for we are not to be saved by the deeds of the law, but by the hearing of faith. No nation is now upon trial for the kingdom. The trial of man in the flesh is at an end. But the sabbath remains to us a moral precept, requiring that we should rest from weekly toil and consecrate the seventh of our time to the public worship of God, and the improvement of our moral and religious nature.

It is indeed true that the observance of the sabbath is nowhere expressly enjoined in the New Testament, and nowhere mentioned, except to redeem it from the austerities imposed upon it by human traditions, or to show that Christians are not to observe it in its legal and Jewish aspect. It is no longer to be regarded as a sign or test of obedience to law in a national trial for the sanctifying of the flesh; but it has the same moral bearing that it had before the law, and under the law. It comes to us as a Divine institution, required by man's nature, and designed for man's benefit. It comes to us sanctioned by the same authority which commands us to worship the only living and true God.

to avoid idolatry and eschew profanity. Christianity does not raise us above the need of the sabbath, it simply changes its legal aspect, and consecrates it to our use in the promotion of our highest and best interests without bringing us into bondage. The sabbath, regarded by the Jew as the sign of the covenant God had made with his nation, and the test of his obedience to that covenant, was invested with an aspect of superstitious dread. He ceased to labor, he rested from his secular business only to feel more severely the bondage of the law. He feared to do any thing on the sabbath, though it were demanded by every consideration of humanity and goodness, lest he should thereby pollute the day and break the covenant. Instead of its being a delight, the sabbath becomes irksome to him. The carnal mind is not subject to the law of God, neither indeed can be. His inward thought was expressed in such language as this, "Behold what a weariness it is! When will the sabbath be gone, that we may buy and sell and get gain?" It was the natural man developed into the morose, unbending Pharisee, striving to compensate for the lack of judgment, mercy, and faith, by the rigidity of his observance of rites and ceremonies, which he felt to be a burden. Such was the Jew who was one outwardly and who served in the oldness of the letter. And to such the sabbath wore an aspect of severity and gloom. Its service was an unwilling tribute paid to an exacting despot. Arraying himself in the habit of a starched formality, he trod with scrupulous exactness the round of its legal ceremonies. Far different was its aspect to the believer—to the one who was a

Jew inwardly—whose delight was in the law of the Lord after the inner man. To him the sabbath was a delight and honorable, and its services were the rejoicing of his soul. And when the lengthening shadows told its departure, he loved to linger in its twilight shades and protract the sweet intercourse he held with God. The natural man, who was laboring to justify himself in the external observance of the law, whose spirituality he understood not, found the sabbath an oppressive burden. And to the natural seed of Abraham, such, in its legal aspect, the sabbath really was—a burden which they were unable to bear, because of the weakness of the flesh. That use of the sabbath, however, ceased on the termination of the trial of the natural seed; and this is perhaps the reason why the observance of the sabbath is nowhere enjoined by express command in the New Testament, as well as a reason why the time of its observance was changed from the seventh day to the first day of the week; circumstances in connection with our subject which require special consideration.

It will not escape the observation of the diligent and careful student of the Scriptures, that the transition from the Jewish dispensation to the Christian was not sudden and violent, but gradual and dispassionate. Jesus merely indicated such a change in his parables and by passing allusions; as for instance in the reference he made to Elijah's being sent to Zarephath or Sarepta to a gentile woman—and also in the parable of the great supper, wherein the first invited guests being found unworthy, the servants were sent forth into the highways and hedges to persuade others to come in.

And He said to his disciples, "I have yet many things to say unto you, but ye cannot bear them now. Howbeit, when he the Spirit of Truth is come, he will guide you into all truth." His parable, that " new wine must not be put into old bottles (skins) else the bottles will burst and the wine be spilled, but new wine must be put into new bottles (skins) and both are preserved," was designed to teach them that his doctrines could not be received by the Jewish mind. Their prejudices were too strong for the reception of the truths concerning the rejection of the natural seed and the calling of the gentiles. Their enlightenment on these points was left to the operation of the facts themselves as evolved in the dispensation of his providence, and to the special influence of the Spirit in connection with those facts. The first Christians were all Jews, or proselytes of Judaism, and were exceedingly zealous of the law. It required a special revelation to induce Peter to go and preach Jesus Christ to Cornelius and his friends who were gentiles. And nothing else but a conviction of his being thus divinely directed by a vision from heaven to do so, silenced the opposition of the circumcision, and extorted the confession, "Then hath God also to the gentiles granted repentance unto life." But so late as the middle of the first century there were many who taught " that it was needful to circumcise" the gentile converts, "and to command them to keep the law of Moses," which being strenuously opposed by Paul, the question was referred to the apostles and elders for their decision.

Now among the peculiarities of the Jewish economy

was the legal use of the sabbath as a sign of their national covenant and a test of their obedience to its requirements. This use had for ages become associated with the seventh day of the week; and any command of Christ or of his apostles to perpetuate the observance of this day would have been almost, if not quite, tantamount to a sanction of its legal use, and would have carried with it, and imposed on the Christian church, the entire burden of the national covenant of which the sabbath was the sign. On this ground I account, and I think satisfactorily, for the absence of any such command. It was not intended that such a use of the sabbath should be continued; for such use was contrary to the genius of the Gospel, and would have subverted the main doctrine of salvation—justification by faith. It would have drawn along with it all the positive and ceremonial observances of Judaism, and have set all men upon seeking justification by the deeds of the law. It might also have imposed upon the church the Rabbinical traditions. The Jewish idea was, that man was made for the sabbath; that the institution was an arbitrary one, to which man was absolutely subjected and which must be observed at any sacrifice of comfort and even of life itself. The example and teaching of Christ was designed to show that the sabbath was made for man, and that it was lawful to do good and promote the comfort, health and well-being of man on that day. He fulfilled the law of the sabbath according to its original constitution, and left us the light of his example and teachings; but gave no command for the observance of the day. In this, also, he appears to have anticipated the change of the day from the seventh to the first of the week, as that on which the sabbath should be observed during the Christian dispensation. There was danger that even in the absence of a command, the continued observance of the same day would have perpetuated its legal use under the law, and thus have imposed upon Christians the covenant of which it was the sign. But the change was not made at once by positive enactment. It was left to the teachings of the Spirit under the facts and revelations of the new dispensation. The Jewish mind was not prepared for the change all at once. It had to be gradually schooled into the new faith, and trained to the new practice.

The first thing, then, was the designation of another day in which Christians should rest from their secular business and attend to their spiritual interests. This was done in the most effective manner by the resurrection of our Lord Jesus Christ from the dead on the morning of the first day of the week. This was the most stupendous fact of redemption, the very foundation of our faith and hope in Christ, and preeminently adapted on account of its reviving, consoling and sanctifying influences to be associated with the sabbath day. During the seventh day of the week, Jesus, the Lord of life and glory, lay dead in the sepulchre. It was to the natural seed their last sabbath, and it was a cancelled one. The day before was the preparation, and, had they received him as their Messiah, it might have been the day of his glorious coronation, and of their exaltation with him in the glory of his kingdom; but instead, they denied him, and desired a murderer to be delivered unto them, and killed the Prince of life, requiring, with loud voices, that he should be crucified. And the soldiers arrayed him in cast-off purple robes, crowned him with an acanthus wreath, put a reed in his hands for a sceptre, and mocked him, bowing the knee and saying, "Hail! King of the Jews!" Then they crucified him, and Jesus, just before he dismissed his spirit, cried, with a loud voice, "It is finished!" The trial of the natural seed was completed. Their unbelief and rejection of him was consummated in that final scene of the mockery and crucifixion. The covenant, which had been broken by generation after generation, was annulled forever. The Aaronic priesthood was abrogated, and the sacrificial rites and offerings for the purifying of the flesh were abolished. The hand-writing of ordinances was nailed to his cross, and the enmity contained therein was taken out of the way. The vail of the temple was rent from top to bottom, and their house was left unto them desolate. And on the seventh day, which symbolized their promised rest, and concerning which God had said, "This is the rest whereby ye may cause the weary to rest, and this is the refreshing, yet they would not hear," the crucified Messiah lay dead in the sepulchre, to indicate that as the sign of their national covenant it was utterly abolished, and that they had failed to attain that which it signified. They were as a nation rejected and their sabbath was at an end. The thing signified was taken from them and the sign was withdrawn. In their estimation that Sabbath was a high day. They had killed the heir and seized on his inheritance. And for fear that his body might be stolen from the sepulchre, they had sealed the stone and set a watch. They rejoiced to think that the only one who seemed to be in the way of their national supremacy and glory was cut off; for they knew not that his death dissolved the relation in which they stood by virtue of the flesh, and transferred the promise of the covenant to the seed of faith, who were, even then, keeping that sabbath in sorrow and dismay. They had trusted that it was he who should have redeemed Israel, but their expectations were cut off with him, and their hopes were sealed up in his tomb. They still thought of national redemption for the natural seed in the flesh. It was therefore a day of rebuke and mourning to them. Their faith in him encouraged them still to look for some light to arise in their obscurity, and in the end of the sabbath, as it began to dawn toward the first day of the week, he rose from the dead. Then they were begotten again to a lively hope. Then life and immortality were illustrated and a new order of things was introduced. And though their question, Wilt thou at this time restore again the kingdom to Israel? indicated that they still indulged some hope of Israel according to the flesh, they soon learned that the flesh was repudiated, and that the children of promise alone were counted for the seed. A new dispensation of grace began, which shone first, indeed, upon Israel, but was designed for all people, and in which the Gospel was to be preached for the obedience of faith among all nations. During this period, the first day of the week, in which all true believers meet for religious worship and spiritual edification, is the divinely instituted sabbath. I say divinely instituted, for it was on the first day that Jesus, having risen from the dead, appeared in the midst of his disciples when they were assembled together, and said, "Peace be unto you." This was the first of a series of weekly manifestations to them upon that day. Nor is it intimated that he ever appeared to them on the seventh day, though they doubtless observed it as the sabbath. Indeed, no further notice is taken of the seventh day as a sabbath in the Gospel, except to show that it is not obligatory on Christians to observe it. The meeting with his disciples on the first day of the week was repeated, no doubt, in order to show that it was not by accident, but designedly, to indicate its substitution as a sabbath instead of the seventh day. And by these weekly manifestations the principle was established, and the disciples continued ever after to meet together, on the first day of the week, for the worship of God and to observe the institutions of Christ. Hence also this day which, on account of Christ's resurrection, and his manifestations thereon, prior to his ascension, was called the Lord's day, was kept as a religious festival, a day of rest from secular business, a sabbath unto the Lord. It was on this day that the Pentecost occurred, and in which the disciples being assembled with one accord in one place, were baptized with the Holy Ghost, and through the ministrations of the word, three thousand were converted to God. It was on this day that they assembled that they might show forth the Lord's death in the breaking of bread, and rejoice together in the hope to which they were begotten again by his resurrection.

By all the early Jewish Christians the seventh day was likewise observed according to the law; hence they kept two sabbaths every week. I say two sabbaths, for the term sabbath was not exclusively applied to the seventh day even under the law, though that was the regularly recurring weekly sabbath of rest. But we find from Lev. xxiii. 24, that the first day of the seventh month was a sabbath, and from Lev. xvi. 31, that the tenth day of the same month was a sabbath, and both of these could not come on the seventh day of the week, and it might frequently happen that neither of them would occur on that day. They were called sabbaths, because they were holy festivals in which secular business was laid aside, and divine services performed. All festivals were so called, and they had not only other sabbatical days besides the seventh day; but they had also sabbatical weeks and sabbatical years. To the early Jewish Christians, then, the first day of the week became a sabbath associated with their faith in Christ and observance of his ordinances. The seventh-day sabbath was altogether associated with their Jewish faith and observance of Jewish rites and ceremonies. The seventh day was their national festival, which they were not yet prepared to relinquish. The first day was their Christian festival which they uniformly observed as a sabbath in honor of Christ. Such was the state of things when the Gospel was first preached to the gentiles.

Now we find that the gentile believers in Christ

were accustomed to meet together on the first day of the week for religious worship, and no mention is made of their ever meeting together on the seventh day. It was on the first day they regularly assembled to commemorate Christ's death in the breaking of bread, and for the ministration of the word and other devotional exercises. It was on the first day of the week, when the disciples at Troas came together to break bread, that Paul preached unto them. He had arrived there on the second day of the week, and abode with them seven days, that he might have the opportunity of spending a Christian sabbath with them, and minister to them the word of salvation. Had they observed the seventh day as a sabbath, doubtless mention would have been made of it, and Paul might have preached to them on that day, as well as on the first day. See Acts xx. 6-7. In writing to the Corinthians, First Epistle, xvi. 1, 2, Paul directs them to put their contributions for the poor saints at Jerusalem, into the treasury on the first day of the week, implying that they were accustomed to meet together on that day, which is, indeed, a fact beyond dispute. It is then a legitimate inference that the gentiles, on their conversion to Christianity, were taught to observe the first day of the week as the sabbath. And hence it has been regarded and observed as such from the beginning of the Christian era.

But the Jewish Christians, who were so zealous of the law, and who said that it was needful that the gentile believers should be circumcised and keep the law of Moses, sought to impose upon them the observance of the seventh day also, and with it the rites and ceremonies of Judaism. This was resolutely resisted by the apostle Paul who, in his letter to the Colossians (ii. 16,) says, "Let no man, therefore, judge you in meat, or in drink, or in respect of a holy day, or of the new moon, or of the sabbath." Here he classes the sabbath, the seventh day of the week, along with other holydays and festivals of the Jewish economy, and exhorts believers to keep free from any superstitious regard to them, as they were only shadows of good things to come, of which Christ is the substance, and not to suffer others to condemn them on account of not observing those institutions of an obsolete economy. This exhortation is also based upon a premise previously stated, that Jesus had " blotted out the hand-writing of ordinances that was against us, which was contrary to us, and took it out of the way, nailing it to his cross." Now this handwriting was the Jewish national covenant of which the sabbath was made the sign. While that covenant remained, it was against the gentiles, who, as long as the trial of the natural seed continued and their covenant was in force, could be partakers of the blessing of the promise, only by becoming proselytes of Judaism. But this hand-writing which was against us was taken away by the death of Christ, which terminated the trial of the natural seed in the flesh, and procured forgiveness of sins and justification for all believers. Hence all who believe in him are justified by faith without the deeds of the law, and are liberated from all obligation to obey the ritual of Judaism, or observe its sabbatical days, months, and years.

And so important was it, that the gentile Christians should stand fast in this liberty wherewith Christ had made them free, that he tells the Galatians (iv. 9–11,) that in consequence of their observance of the sacred festivals of Judaism, in compliance with the instructions of the Judaizing teacher, he was afraid of them lest he had bestowed upon them labor in vain: for by turning from the Gospel liberty to the seventh-day sabbath and other Jewish observances, they plainly declared that they were seeking to be justified by the works of the law, and were fallen from grace.

The apostle did not interfere with the Jewish Christians in their continued regard for the seventh day and their practice of other Jewish rites. He only withstood the attempt of the zealots of law to impose that burden upon the gentiles. The Jew who believed in Christ might deem it expedient still to carry the burden; but there was no propriety in forcing it upon the gentiles, seeing "that a man is not justified by the works of the law, but by the faith of Jesus Christ." It had been definitely settled at Jerusalem, on the question concerning circumcision, that no such burden should be imposed on them who from among the gentiles had turned to God; and that Paul, having been called of God to that special ministry, should go to the gentiles and regulate the religious institutions to be observed by them according to the Gospel which he had received of our Lord Jesus Christ; and that the other apostles should have the regulation of the ordinances and customs to be observed by the circumcision. Hence in his letter to the Romans (xiv. 5, 6,) he says, "One man (the Jewish Christian) esteemeth one day (the seventh) above another: another man (the gentile Christian) esteemeth every day alike. Let every many be fully persuaded in his own mind. He that regardeth the day (the seventh) regardeth it unto the Lord; and he that regardeth not the day (the seventh), to the Lord he regardeth it not." Those Jewish believers who held the seventh day as sacred and observed it as a sabbath, did so out of regard to the command of God in relation to their national covenant. It was far better that they should do so than that they should violate their conscience. But the gentiles, with whom no such national covenant was made, esteemed every day alike, and hence did not attach any sacredness to the seventh day, and did not observe it as the sabbath; feeling satisfied in their mind that the moral precept in respect to the sanctification of one day out of every seven for religious purposes and rest from secular business, was as acceptably obeyed in the observance of the first day of the week as on the seventh. And they observed the first instead of the seventh, out of regard to the authority of the Lord of the sabbath, by whom the change of the day had been designated. We thus learn that the command of the decalogue which requires us to remember the sabbath day to keep it holy, is no less applicable to the first day of the week or the Lord's day under the Christian dispensation than it was to the seventh day under the Jewish dispensation. The apostle's argument being not against the keeping of the sabbath, which is a moral precept; but in vindication of the gentile Christians who observed the first day of the week, and not the seventh, as their sabbath. It is probable that the Jewish Christians observed the seventh day as well as the first until the destruction of Jerusalem, when the nationality of Israel was destroyed, after which the seventh day ceased to be observed by even the Jewish Christians, and the first day received the name of the sabbath, and has ever since continued to be observed as such by the Christian church.

Thus the change of the day is satisfactorily accounted for, and the reason for it abundantly sufficient. The manner, too, in which the change was effected is seen to be in accordance with the Divine wisdom and grace, for the salvation of the greatest number of both Jews and gentiles. The Jewish Christians, as long as their temple stood, and their nationality lasted, were allowed to practice their rites and observe the institutions of Judaism, and many thousands of them consequently believed in Christ, and were saved. And the gentile Christians being exempt from the burdens of the Jewish ritual, the more readily embraced the hope set before them in the Gospel. At length the Jewish economy vanished away with its rites and ceremonies, its days and months and years, and the Lord's day or the first day of the week was alone retained as the Christian sabbath—a day of rest from secular business—a day of sacred and spiritual exercises designed to sanctify and save. It is therefore incumbent on all the followers of Christ, who acknowledge him as Lord, to observe this day as a divine institution. The profanation of it, by the transaction of worldly business thereon, is an immorality according to the ethics of the Gospel. The due observance of it is necessary for the great work of human redemption. The sabbath was made for man. Made to promote his highest interests and sublimest pleasures. And such is the object of the Christian sabbath; a day whose associations are of the most pure and ennobling nature, and which, if observed in faith, is adapted to secure the spiritual enlightenment and moral improvement of man. As a day of rest merely, it would not answer the design of its institution. But it is not without its appropriate services. Its sacred hours are not to be spent in idleness. It is redemption's working-day, and to this great purpose it is consecrated. Christianity is a system of religious faith and practice; one of the dispensations of grace to man, for whose benefit the sabbath was made. This system has its religious services, in which the knowledge of salvation is imparted, and growth in grace is secured. Forsake not the assembling of yourselves together, is an exhortation which relates specially to their publicly assembling upon the first day of the week. This is one of the chief uses of the sabbath. On it the people of God were wont to meet for his worship, for the observance of his ordinances, and for Christian fellowship. Our religious improvement and edification demand zealous and regular attention to the means of grace instituted in the church. Whoever neglects them retards his progress in the knowledge of the Lord. Yea, he resigns his hope of reward in the kingdom of God; for when the world by wisdom knew not God, it pleased God through the foolishness of preaching to save them that believe. The due observance of this day is pretty correct evidence of the religious state of the Christian. Few if any really love the sabbath and rest according to the commandment, unless they have true piety. The neglect of the sabbath is the characteristic of those who fear not God, or whose religion is sadly declining.

John, the beloved disciple, says, "I was in the spirit on the Lord's day." And this signifies to us the way to profit by its holy services of prayer and praise and meditation in God's word. To render the sabbath a delight and honorable, we must perform our religious duties in the newness of the spirit, and not in the oldness of the letter.

It is this spirituality of worship which gives it the power to sanctify and bless. The sabbath is a blessing to them who are in the spirit. In the early morn they hail its sacred light in sweet communings with the Father of all: they walk with him all day in the ordinances of religion; and at night, with hearts overflowing with love, they linger in its departing shadow to pour out their thanksgiving to God for the sweet and heavenly peace its sacred hours distil.

> "The day that God hath blessed,
> Comes tranquilly on with its welcome rest.
> It speaks of Creation's early bloom;
> It speaks of the prince who burst the tomb.
> Then summon the spirit's exalted powers,
> And devote to heaven the hallowed hours."

CHAPTER III.

THE MILLENNIUM'S SYMBOL-DAY.

"And he said unto them, The sabbath was made for man, and not man for the sabbath. Therefore the Son of Man is Lord also of the sabbath."—Mark ii. 27, 28.

THE sabbath is the Millennium's symbol-day. Known unto God are all his works from the beginning of the world; and in making a revelation of his purposes to man, he has made the institutions and laws of one age to be the symbols and prophecies of a succeeding age. This is a remarkable and important feature of Bible truth, too commonly overlooked. The Passover, while it was actually commemorative of the redemption of the first-born of Israel from the sword of the destroying angel, in the night that God brought forth his people out of Egypt, was also designed as a symbol of the redemption of the Church of the first-born, whose names are written in heaven, by the blood of Christ, our passover, who was sacrificed for us. And the law that not a bone of the paschal lamb should be broken, was designed as a prediction that not a bone of Christ's body should be broken by the soldiers when they broke the legs of the two malefactors who were crucified along with him. In like manner, the sabbath is not only commemorative of the rest of Jehovah from his works of creation, and sanctified as a day of grace to man in the economy of redemption, but it is also a symbol of that rest which remaineth unto the people of God. It is hence termed a shadow of good things to come. This use of the sabbath was supralapsarian. It presented this symbolic aspect to Adam while yet in innocency; for as he was then under a covenant of works, it intimated to him, that as God had rested from his works in the seventh day, so, on condition of his continued obedience, should he and his obedient posterity rest from their works on the seventh millennary of the World. When God created man, he made him to have dominion over the earth, and put all things under his feet. Dominion, however, was conferred upon him, not absolutely, but conditionally. Mankind were to be multiplied—the earth populated, subdued and governed; and, on condition of continued obedience, he was to be confirmed in holiness and established in the perpetual sovereignty of earth; and his obedient posterity would in like manner have become associated with him in the government. These works would have required six thousand years, of which God's works of creation for six days was a symbol; and, then, as on the seventh day, God rested from his works, so should man have rested from his on the seventh Millennary of the world. Hence Paul, in Heb. iv. 3, speaks of that rest or Millennial sabbath as having being designed from the foundation of the world. The preparatory works were finished in the symbol week of Creation, and the rest itself introduced in the first holy symbol sabbath. This was the expressive manner in which God was pleased to declare or make known his purpose and plan. And as Adam was created in the image of God in knowledge, he doubtless was acquainted with the meaning of these symbolic facts. Thus, in the original constitution of the world, the sabbath was set forth as a symbol of that state of holiness, happiness and glory, to which man might have attained by continued obedience to the Divine law; but of which he fell short by transgression,

> "Till one greater man
> Restore us, and regain the blissful seat."

Adam, the first representative man, failed to keep the law, or to continue in obedience. He sinned and forfeited all. But God's purpose has not failed, because Adam failed; nor has the symbol sabbath of creation lost its signification. The necessity of divine interposition was foreseen, and adequate provision was determined upon for the redemption of man. Help was laid on one mighty to save. A second representative man was provided, and Christ Jesus, the Son of God, will, through the remedial system of grace, effect what Adam failed to attain through the covenant of works. Hence, Jesus said, "My Father worketh hitherto, and I work." This was an answer to the cavils of the Jews, who said that he had broken the sabbath by healing the impotent man who lay by the pool of Bethesda waiting for the moving of the waters. It seems intended to convey to their minds the idea that from the fall of man until then the Father had been engaged in a great work—the work of human redemption, for which the sabbath was an appropriate day, a day set apart from secular business and specially devoted thereto—and that his work was identically the same as that of the Father's. Indeed, it was by him the Father wrought in all his operations, and whatever he did was the Father's work, for he did nothing of himself; he was simply performing the work which the Father sent him to do. The entire plan was laid down by the Father, and he did nothing but what he saw in the plan. Hence he says, John iv. 34, "My meat is to do the will of him that sent me, and to finish his work." It was not only admissible, therefore, but absolutely right, and in accordance with the design of the day, that he should be employed in doing those works of benevolence and mercy, which were not merely intended to alleviate human suffering, but to furnish unquestionable evidence of his mission, and lay the foundation of that faith in him which saves to the uttermost. In this day, and by its divine services, God is still working with men and in men to will and to do of his good pleasure, while they, by faith in and obedience to the Gospel, are actively working out their own salvation with fear and trembling. Not that all men will be saved by this Divine working; for all men do not believe the word of God nor obey him. Only believers are thus saved; "For this is the work of God," said Jesus, "that ye believe on him whom he hath sent." And faith in Jesus is productive of holiness and salvation. This work of redemption is still progressing, and will occupy the six millenniums symbolized by the six days work of creation, and the seventh millennium will then be the great sabbath of the earth.

The sabbath, as the Millennium's symbol day, has been associated with the work of redemption from its commencement. There is no scripture warrant for supposing that Adam was ignorant of the original constitution of the world, and the relations, duties, and responsibilities belonging to himself as the first representative man. He was created in knowledge. This cannot mean that he was created in ignorance. He knew all that it was important for him to know. And when he had transgressed the law, and involved himself and his posterity in sin and death, he was still fully competent to understand the import of those terms in which God was pleased to make known his glorious purpose of redemption. The declaration that the seed of the woman should bruise the serpent's head, could not have been the foundation of faith; nor could it have afforded any comfort of hope, unless it were understood. And if understood, as we have every reason to believe it was, then its bearing upon the subject of our discourse was apprehended, and hope must have anticipated that the six thousand years of redemption would terminate in the restitution of all things and an everlasting rest.

That one day is with the Lord as a thousand years, and a thousand years as one day, was not only understood from the symbolic use of the days of Creation, and the first sabbath, but also from the use of the term day in the penalty annexed to the command that they should not eat of the fruit of the tree of the knowledge of good and evil, viz.: "In the day thou eatest thereof thou shalt surely die." Here the term day did not refer to a natural day of twenty-four hours; for Adam did not die in the natural or solar day in which he transgressed: but it refers to a millennial day of a thousand years, within which Adam did die. This is proved from the reference to it in the ninetieth Psalm: "Thou turnest man to destruction, and sayest, Return ye children of men. For a thousand years in thy sight are but as yesterday when it is passed, and as a watch in the night." This evidently refers to the sentence pronounced upon man, "Dust thou art and unto dust shalt thou return." This is the sentence by which man was turned to destruction, and this sentence was to be executed in the day in which man transgressed; that is, within a thousand years, which with the Lord is counted as a day. In the antediluvian age there were probably no deaths in infancy and childhood, and the people generally lived to be several hundred years old. They doubtless understood that the penalty of death, which had passed upon all men on account of Adam's sin, would be executed within the period of a thousand years. Adam himself lived nine hundred and thirty years, nearly three-fifths of the antediluvian age, and hence could instruct his posterity in relation to the original constitution of the world, and the work of redemption, in both of which the sabbath and its symbolic signification was an important feature. Besides, during that age, the garden of Eden still existed, and the cherub with the flaming sword kept the way of the tree of life; thus insuring the execution of the penalty by debarring man from the only means by which his life could be protracted. And the Lord himself, who dwelt in the garden, appeared to his worshipers, as occasion required, to accept the sacrifices of faith, and to administer judgment in righteousness, making known the way of salvation through faith and voluntary obedience. In the prophecy of Enoch (Jude 14), we have evidence that, during that age, there were divine revelations concerning the glorious advent of the Lord to the earth, and the participation of the saints in the rest or sabbath of redemption which he will then introduce. "Behold the Lord cometh, with ten thousands of his saints, to execute judgment upon all, and to convince all that are ungodly among them, of all their ungodly deeds which they have ungodly committed, and of all their hard speeches which ungodly sinners have spoken against him." This prophecy indicates that when he comes for these purposes, his saints, who shall all have been previously redeemed and glorified, shall come with him, and being constituted associate judges or magistrates, shall enter with him into that kingdom and glory then to be revealed. The translation of Enoch, as the seventh from Adam, was probably designed to teach that the bodies of all the saints shall be changed, that they may be fashioned like unto Christ's most glorious body, when he comes to establish his kingdom in the seventh millenary of the world.

After the Flood, the kingdom of Melchisedek was divinely constituted a type of the coming kingdom of heaven, or the millennial reign of the Son of God; and the sabbath, as then observed, was doubtless a symbol of that rest thus shadowed forth. In the promise to Abraham, further revelation was made of the Divine purpose; and he, and Isaac, and Jacob, heirs with him of the same promise, sojourned as strangers and pilgrims in the land which they should, in the future, receive as an inheritance; and died in faith, not having received the fulfillment of the promise; but believing in its certainty, and looking forward to a time when they shall be raised from the dead in immortal and glorified bodies, and possess the land forever. They looked for a city whose builder and maker is God. But without stopping to dwell upon these points particularly, I invite your attention to the fact that the Jewish people entertained the expectation of the Millennium long before the Christian era. There was among them the tradition of the house of Elias, "That the world shall endure six thousand years: two thousand void of the law, two thousand under the law, and two thousand the days of the Messiah; and that the seventh is the sabbath, and is the beginning of the world to come." They held that the six thousand years would correspond with the six days work of creation, and that the seventh thousand would correspond with the sabbath—a season of holy rest and divine benefaction. Hence some persons have termed the millenarian theory a Jewish superstition, as if every thing Jewish was to be repudiated. They have done this apparently without reflecting that to the Jews were committed the sacred oracles, and that the Millennium has for its foundation the glorious promises made to the Fathers, and so sweetly and sublimely celebrated in the songs of the prophet poets. To the pious Jew the sabbath was not only a day of rest from toil and care, but also a sign or symbol of that latter day of glory and blessedness embraced in the promise to Abraham, and which he saw depicted in such glowing colors in the language of the prophets. He contemplated each succeeding sabbath as a renewed symbol of the promised rest which he apprehended by faith. Every believing Jew was a spiritual man—an Israelite indeed—and to him the rites and ceremonies of Judaism were no more gross than are the outward ordinances of Christianity to the believer now. "To the pure all things are pure; but to them that are defiled and unbelieving nothing is pure." Noble examples have we of those early saints who all died in faith, not having received the promise, God having reserved some better thing for us, that they, without us, should not be made perfect. And from those olden times we hear the chiming of the symbol sabbath bells, struck by the hammer of faith, reverberating among the hills of prophecy, and awakening within us the hope of everlasting rest.

The future rest of the people of God, or the Millennium, is one of the principal topics of Paul's letter to the Hebrews, cautioning them against the like unbelief which excluded their fathers, who were brought out of Egypt, from entering into the promised land, saying, "Let us therefore fear, lest a promise being left us of entering into his rest, any of you should seem to come short of it. For unto us was the Gospel preached as well as unto them; but the word did not profit them, not beng mixed with faith in them that heard it. For we which believe do enter into rest, as he said, As I have sworn in my wrath, if they shall enter into my rest, although the works were finished from the foundation of the world. For he spake in a certain place of the seventh day on this wise, And God did rest the seventh day from all his works. And in this place again, If they shall enter into my rest. Seeing therefore it remaineth that some must enter therein, and they to whom it was first preached entered not in because of unbelief; let us, therefore, labor to enter into that rest, lest any man fall after the same example of unbelief." In this passage the apostle shows that there is a promised rest; and that it was symbolized by God's resting on the seventh day from his works of creation. This rest was promised to Israel in the flesh on condition of their keeping the covenant; but they entered not in because of unbelief. The national covenant was broken, and the promise is confirmed with believers only. For we who believe do enter in. We enter in by faith, which is the substance of things hoped for. Or, as in scripture, the present tense is frequently put for the future to show the certainty of the thing, we who believe shall enter in. It is ours by promise now, and shall be ours in reality hereafter. For this rest remaineth unto the people of God. It is yet future.

But, he continues: "Again he limiteth a certain day, saying in David, To-day, after so long a time; as it is said, To-day if ye will hear his voice, harden not your hearts. For if Jesus had given them rest, then would he not afterward have spoken of another day. There remaineth therefore a rest"—a sabbatism—the keeping of a sabbath—"unto the people of God." Herein he shows that the rest spoken of is yet future. It was indeed preached to Israel in the wilderness, but they entered not in because of unbelief; for God said that they should not enter into that rest. And when he brought their children into the land of promise, still they, being disobedient like their fathers, were not brought into that rest, seeing that a long time afterward, even in David's time, he still speaks of that rest as future. Nor did any generation of Israel enter in; for they all disobeyed God, and kept not his covenant and polluted his sabbaths, and therefore were nationally excluded from that rest. The rest then is one not yet possessed. It is future. It yet remains unto the people of God. This rest is, then, the seventh millenary—the keeping of a sabbath after the work of redemption shall be finished in the salvation of the church of the first-born whose names are written in heaven. This rest includes the blessings of the covenant made with Abraham and his seed: and shall be given to all who believe in Christ and keep his commandments. The seed of faith shall enter in: for if ye are Christ's then are ye Abraham's seed and heirs according to the promise. So then they that are of faith shall be blessed with faithful Abraham.

"And he that hath entered into his rest, he also hath ceased from his own works, as God did from his." This cannot mean that he ceases from laboring to enter in through the deeds of the law; for that does not accord with the comparison employed to illustrate it. We cannot compare the works of an unbeliever

—sinful works—with the works of God. The passage is to be understood of the believers actually entering into that millennial rest; for he will then have truly ceased from all his work and labor in this preparatory state. The work of redemption will then be finished: and the whole redeemed and glorified church will enter into that rest at once. The argument of the apostle is conclusive in regard to the futurity of that rest; it is, He that hath entered into his rest hath ceased from his works; but believers have not yet ceased from their works, hence they have not yet entered into that rest. The rest is yet to come. Hence the voice which the beloved disciple heard in the Isle of Patmos, said, "Blessed are the dead which die in the Lord from henceforth, yea, saith the Spirit, that that they may rest from their labors, and their works do follow them." And the time of this rest is shown by the context to be when the one hundred forty and four thousand of Israel, representing the redeemed from the earth shall stand with the Lamb on Mount Zion; when, indeed, the harvest of the earth shall be reaped, and all the saints of God shall be glorified with Jesus Christ. And therefore it is to be at the second coming of Christ, at the end of the present dispensation, to establish his millennial kingdom: for then shall the Lord recompense tribulation to the troublers of his church, but rest to them that are troubled.

The early Christians all believed in this future rest, and held substantially the same view respecting the sabbath as a symbol of it. Thus Barnabas, in the first century, comments upon the words of Moses: "And God made in six days the works of his hands, and he finished them on the seventh day, and he rested in it and sanctified it. Consider, children, what that signifies, 'He finished them in six days.' This it signifies, that the Lord will finish all things in six thousand years. For a day with him is a thousand years, as he himself testifies, saying, 'Behold this day shall be a thousand years.' Therefore, children, in six days, that is, in six thousand years, shall all things be consummated. 'And he rested the seventh day.' This signifies that when his Son shall come, and shall abolish the season of the wicked one, and shall judge the ungodly, and shall change the sun, and the moon, and the stars, then he shall rest gloriously in that seventh day." Barnabas "was a good man, full of the Holy Spirit and of faith." He was a companion of the apostles. He first introduced Paul to Peter and the other apostles, and labored with him in preaching the Gospel. His opinion corresponds with Paul's language on this point, and is entitled to great weight. His views evidently coincide with and are derived from the scriptures. As for instance, Isa. xxx. 26, "Moreover, the light of the moon shall be as the light of the sun, and the light of the sun shall be seven-fold as the light of seven days, in the day that the Lord bindeth up the breach of his people, and healeth the stroke of their wound." And xxiv. 23. "Then shall the moon be confounded and the sun ashamed when the Lord of hosts shall reign in Mount Zion and in Jerusalem, and before his ancients gloriously." With these predictions he associated the second coming of the Son of Man which precedes his reign, and taught that the seventh millenary shall be the great sabbath of the world in which Christ and his glorified saints shall reign over all the earth.

Justin Martyr, in the second century, declares that the Millenarian Theory was believed by all true Christians in his day. It was not an opinion of secondary importance; but a leading and cardinal doctrine of the church. He admits that some who professed to be Christians did not acknowledge it; but he says they were such as did not follow godly and pure doctrine. "But," says he, "I, and as many as are orthodox Christians in all respects, do acknowledge that there shall be a resurrection of the flesh, and a residence of a thousand years in Jerusalem, rebuilt, and adorned, and enlarged, as the prophets Ezekiel, Isaiah and others unanimously attest." He quotes from Isa. lxv. the promise of a new heaven and a new earth as applicable to the Millennium, and also the scripture, "One day with the Lord is a thousand years." "Moreover," says he, "a certain man among us, whose name was John, being one of the twelve apostles of Christ, in that revelation which was shown to him, prophesied, that those who believe in Christ shall live a thousand years in the new Jerusalem." He also says, "We may judge from many places in scripture, that those are in the right who say six thousand years is the time fixed for the duration of the present frame (condition) of the world." The allusion here is to the symbolic character of the six days' creation, and the sabbath, as a divine method of indicating the cycles of redemption and the sabbath of millennium blessedness.

Cyprian, also, bears a similar testimony. He

fixes the period of six thousand years for the world's age, and the dissolution of the present state of things, and speaks of the seventh millennium as the consummation of all, and the rest of God's people.

Lactantius, in the fourth century, says, "Because all the works of God were finished in six days, it is necessary that the world shall remain in this state six ages, that is six thousand years." And again: "Because, having finished the works, he rested on the seventh day and blessed it, it is necessary that the end of the six thousandth year all wickedness shall be abolished out of the earth, and justice shall reign for a thousand years." Again: "When the Son of God shall have destroyed injustice, and shall have restored the just to life, he shall be conversant among men a thousand years, and shall rule them with most just government."

Such were the views entertained by the primitive Christians when "the style of Christianity was to believe, to do, and to suffer." In all their tribulation and persecutions they were comforted and supported by the blessed hope of that rest which remaineth to the people of God. They understood it to be the Divine purpose, as symbolized by the six days of creation and the sabbath, to accomplish in six thousand years, which were foreseen as necessary thereto, the redemption of an elect people consisting of all true believers, to save and glorify them, and with them to rest gloriously in the seventh thousand, when all wicked governments being destroyed, the saints shall take the kingdom and possess it forever and ever.

The sabbath is the Millennium's symbol-day. The sabbath in Eden at the close of the six days' work of creation was its most perfect type. It was man's first day of holy and joyous life; and was given to him as a symbol of that everlasting rest in which, after six millenaries of preparation in populating and subjecting the earth, he, if faithful, and all his obedient and sanctified offspring, should be immortalized and glorified, and established in perpetual sovereignty over the earth. And when man had sinned, and was driven from the garden of Eden, the sabbath was continued to him as a symbol of the rest to be obtained through faith in the seed of the woman, who shall bruise the serpent's head, and at the close of six thousand years of working for human redemption, shall, with his immortalized and glorified saints, establish his everlasting kingdom of righteousness and peace upon earth. And, through all ages and dispensations, and to the believing in every generation, to Abel and Enoch and Noah, and Shem and Abraham, and all the seed of faith, the sabbath, in its sacred rest from worldly toil, and with its Divine services of grateful, loving worship, has told of a coming day of blessedness and glory. The sabbath, as the prophetic tongue of time, has spoken in the language of mercy and grace to the weary, restless pilgrims of earth, bidding them seek, in fellowship with the Lord, an everlasting rest, in the future restitution of all things. During the trial of the natural seed of Abraham, while it was a sign to them of a special covenant which as a nation they broke in every period of their trial, and so failed of attaining to the glory and blessedness it symbolized, it was to the true Israel a symbol of the rest remaining to the people of God on the terms of a better covenant: and the pious Jew looked forward to the coming of the Messiah, when Abraham and all believers, being raised and immortalized, shall be brought into that rest. And when the trial of the natural seed was ended, and for sufficient reasons the first day of the week superseded the seventh as the sabbath, it retained all its symbolical import, and, to the humble Christian, speaks of the rest that remaineth unto the people of God.

As the Millennium's symbol-day the sabbath is to be highly esteemed. It turns our thoughts from the turmoil and sorrow of the present, to the peace and joy of the future. It affords us time and opportunity to hear and meditate upon the word of God, and make preparation for the inheritance of the saints in light. McCheyne says: "When a believer lays aside his pen or loom, brushes aside his worldly cares, leaving them behind him with his week-day clothes, and comes up to the house of God, it is like the morning of the resurrection, the day when we shall come out of great tribulation, into the presence of God and the Lamb. When he sits under the preached word, and hears the voice of the Shepherd leading and feeding his soul, it reminds him of the day when the Lamb that is in the midst of the throne shall feed him and lead him to living fountains of waters. When he joins in the psalm of praise, it reminds him of the day when his hands shall strike the harp of God" in the assembly of the saints, where the sabbath has no end.

> "Hail, holy day! The blessing from above
> Brightens thy presence like a smile of love,
> Soothing, like oil upon a troubled sea,
> The roughest waves of human destiny—
> Cheering the good, and to the poor oppressed
> Bearing the promise of their heavenly rest"
>
> Mrs. Hale.

CHAPTER IV.

THE LORD OF THE SABBATH.

" And he said unto them, The sabbath was made for man, and not man for the sabbath. Therefore the Son of man is Lord also of the Sabbath."—Mark ii. 27, 28.

THE term Son of man, in the New Testament, is expressly appropriated to Jesus Christ, and seems intended to intimate his conditional affinity to our race, assumed for the purpose of redemption. The incarnation of the Son of God is a great mystery: a fact in theology which commands our faith, although it exceeds our comprehension. It is a prime truth in revelation, a foundation-stone of the Christian system. "When the fullness of time was come, God sent forth his Son, made of a woman, made under the law, to redeem them that were under the law; that we might receive the adoption of sons." This must be regarded as an essential truth of revelation, without which the Gospel would possess no power to save. To this the doctrine of Christ crucified owes all its moral influence. It was not, therefore, in vain curiosity that Jesus asked his disciples the question, "Whom do men say that I, the Son of Man, am?" But it was to make it the occasion of impressive discrimination between human opinions and a Divine revelation concerning his nature and relations. The answer discloses to us the prevailing humanitarianism of the day. "Some say that thou art John the Baptist; some, Elias; and others, Jeremiah, or one of the prophets." Nicodemus had said, "We know that thou art a teacher come from God; for no man can do the miracles which thou doest, except God be with him." But the highest conception which the Jewish people generally entertained respecting him was, that he was one of the old prophets who had risen from the dead, or as one of the prophets. Their notions were all humanitarian, and were derived from no higher source than their own vain reasoning. On the contrary, when, in reply to the question, "Whom say ye that I am?" Peter answered, "Thou art the Christ the Son of the living God," Jesus pronounced it a Divine revelation — an inspired oracle — saying, "Blessed art thou, Simon, son of Jonah, for flesh and blood hath not revealed it unto thee, but my Father who is in Heaven." And this agrees with another declaration of his, "No man knoweth the Son, but the Father." The humanitarian scheme cannot stand in the face of these declarations. If Jesus were simply a human being, conceived and born as other men, there was nothing in regard to his nature requiring a special revelation to make him known. If Jesus were simply a human being, the most of his sayings in relation to himself are sheer nonsense or blasphemous assumption. Take for instance, John iii. 13, "No man hath ascended up into heaven, but he that came down from heaven, even the Son of man who is in heaven;" and John vi. 62, "What and if ye shall see the Son of man ascend up where he was before?"

These passages show that no man, no one of Adam's race, ever ascended into heaven that he should come down from heaven, and hence the Son of man, who came down from heaven, is of heaven—one whose nature and origin are heavenly and divine. And when he ascended up into heaven, it was to return to the place and condition which he had previously occupied and enjoyed.

The semi-humanitarian scheme is but little, if any better than the humanitarian: for although it admits the doctrine of the miraculous conception of Jesus, yet it maintains that he was only a human being, and denies any previous existence to him who was born of the Virgin. It holds that he was merely a human being, supernaturally conceived, or miraculously created, and first began to exist about eighteen hundred and fifty-nine years ago. The only differences between the humanitarian and the semi-humanitarian schemes are these: The former rejects the doctrine of the miraculous conception; the latter admits it. The former maintains that God is but one person; the latter maintains that he is three persons. The former believes that God himself was in special union with the human being Jesus; the latter believes that only one of the three persons of the compound Godhead was in special union with the human being Jesus. Both systems agree in denying the previous existence of the Son of man; they deny that the Son of man came down from heaven; they deny that when the Son of man ascended up into heaven, he returned to a place and condition he had previously occupied and enjoyed. We are compelled, therefore, in fidelity to the word of God, the revelation which God has given us concerning his Son Jesus Christ, to reject both these systems as erroneous, as the offspring of human speculation and unbelief. Our inquiry is, "What saith the Scriptures?" Our faith must not stand in the wisdom of men, but in the Divine testimony; and,

First. The Scriptures teach us that he who is called the Son of man, is really the Son of the living God. This was the amount of Peter's answer to the question of Jesus, and expressly sanctioned by our Lord as a divinely revealed truth, known only by inspiration of God. When the angel Gabriel announced to Mary the conception of Jesus, he said, "The Holy Spirit shall come upon thee, and the power of the Highest shall overshadow thee; therefore, also, that holy thing which shall be born of thee shall be called the Son of God." Luke ii. 35. Here the name Son of God is given to the Virgin's child, to him who was born in Bethlehem. At the Feast of the Dedication, as Jesus walked in Solomon's porch, the Jews came to him and said, "How long dost thou make us doubt? If thou be the Christ, tell us plainly." Jesus answered, "I told you and ye believed not: the works that I do in my Father's name, they bear witness of me. But ye believe not, because ye are not of my sheep, as I said unto you. My sheep hear my voice, and I know them and they follow me; and I give unto them eternal life, and they shall never perish, neither shall any pluck them out of my hand. My Father, who gave them me, is greater than all; and none is able to pluck them out of my Father's hand. I and my Father are one." Then the Jews took up stones to stone him as they said, for blasphemy, because that, being a man, he made himself God. Jesus answered, "Is it not written in your law, I said, ye are Gods? If he called them Gods to whom the word of God came, and the Scriptures cannot be broken, say ye of him whom the Father hath sanctified and sent into the world, Thou blasphemest, because I said, I am the Son of God? If I do not the works of my Father, believe me not. But if I do, though ye believe not me, believe the work; that ye may know and believe that the Father is in me, and I in him." John x. 22-38. I have selected these passages, because they prove beyond all cavil, that Jesus is the Son of God; because they have reference to the Man Christ Jesus, to him who was made of a woman, made under the law, made in the likeness of sinful flesh, and was found in fashion as a man; because, without supposing a gross deception, they cannot be construed to apply to any Divine person other than himself, either in union with him or dwelling in him. The hypothesis that there were two natures, or rather two persons—a divine person and a human person—combined in the Messiah, and that he sometimes spake of himself and his relations in reference to each of these persons separately, or that sometimes he spake as God and sometimes as man, is resorted to for the purpose of reconciling the incongruities which his language presents to the semi-humanitarian scheme. It is, however, without any foundation in Scripture; not being as much as intimated in the Gospels or the Epistles, but is contrary to the tenor of Christ's teaching and to the sincerity and candor of his character. The supposition that he thus spake without apprising his auditors of such a distinction, represents him as disingenuous, as sporting with the ignorance, and shocking the religious sense of the people; and robs his defense of himself from the charge of blasphemy of all pertinence and reason. The term Son of God is understood by some semi-humanitarians to apply to the Divine person, and by others to the human person of the Messiah. The former maintain that the distinction on which it is founded exists essentially in the Godhead; the latter ridicule the idea of an eternal Son, and maintain that the foundation for it exists only in the manhood. The passages I have quoted refer to no such distinction; but simply teach us that Jesus Christ is the Son of God. Other passages could be adduced, but these are sufficient.

Second. The Scriptures teach that the Son of man existed before he came into the world, and also before any thing was created. In John viii. 23, it is recorded that Jesus said to the Jews, "Ye are from beneath; I am from above: ye are of this world, I am not of this world." Again, v. 42, "If God were your Father ye would love me, for I proceeded forth and came from God; neither came I of myself, but he sent me." And when they asked him, v. 53, "Art thou greater than our father Abraham, who is dead? and the prophets are dead; whom makest thou thyself?" Jesus answered, (vv. 54-58,) "If I honor myself, my honor is nothing: it is my Father that honoreth me, of whom ye say that he is your God; yet ye have not known him, but I know him; and if I should say, I know him not, I should be a liar like unto you: but

I know him and keep his saying. Your father Abraham rejoiced to see my day: and he saw it, and was glad. Then said the Jews to him, Thou art not yet fifty years old, and hast thou seen Abraham? Jesus said unto them, Verily, verily, I say unto you, Before Abraham was, I am." Again in his prayer, John xvii. 5, Jesus says, And now, O Father, glorify thou me with thine own self, with the glory that I had with thee before the world was." These passages show unequivocally that Jesus claimed for himself, as he then appeared before his auditors, a heavenly origin; that he, as the Son of God, proceeded forth and came from God, and hence that he existed before Abraham, yea, before the world was made. The term "proceeded forth," evidently relates to his nature as the Son of God, and is equivalent to the phrase "only begotten of the Father:" and the term "came from," relates to his mission as the Messiah, and is equivalent to the phrase that the Father sent him. No language could more clearly set forth his pre-existence. The doctrine taught in these passages fully accords with what the personal Wisdom, or Son of God, is represented as saying in Prov. viii. 22–30, "The Lord possessed me in the beginning of his way, before his works of old. I was set up from everlasting, from the beginning, or ever the earth was. When there were no depths I was brought forth; when there were no fountains abounding with water. Before the mountains were settled, before the hills was I brought forth. While as yet he had not made the earth, nor the fields, nor the highest parts of the dust of the world. When he prepared the heavens I was there; when he set a compass upon the face of the depths; when he established the clouds above; when he strengthened the fountains of the deep; when he gave to the sea his decree, that the waters should not pass his commandment; when he appointed the foundations of the earth; then I was by him, as one brought up with him; and I was daily his delight, rejoicing always before him."

Third. The Scriptures teach that he is the personal representative of God. He is called "The image of God," 2 Cor. iv. 4; "The image of the invisible God," Col. i. 15; "The brightness of his glory and the express image of his person," Heb. i. 3; because it is in him and by him that God manifests himself to his creatures. The invisible could not be otherwise manifested without a representative. God therefore has his image, or representative, and that image is his Son. "No man hath seen God at any time; the only-begotten Son who is in the bosom of the Father, he hath declared him," John i. 18; that is, hath, as his representative, proclaimed him and otherwise made him known. So in the first verse, "In the beginning was the Word, and the Word was with God, and the Word was God." I understand the last clause to mean that the Word represented God; as when Paul says "that rock was Christ," he means that rock represented Christ. The Son of God is a necessity of the Divine Nature—necessary to the manifestation of the being, perfections and personality of God. As it is written, "No man knoweth the Son, but the Father; neither knoweth any man the Father, but the Son, and he to whom the Son will reveal him." Hence

Christ is the "only-begotten Son of God"—"the first-born of every creature"—"the beginning of the creation of God." And by him God is made known to all intelligences. It was as the representative of God that Jesus, in answer to Philip's request, "Lord, show us the Father and it sufficeth us," said, "Have I been so long time with you, and yet hast thou not known me, Philip? He that hath seen me hath seen the Father, and how sayest thou, then, Show us the Father? Believest thou not that I am in the Father and the Father in me? The words that I speak unto you, I speak not of myself; but the Father that dwelleth in me, he doth the works. Believe me that I am in the Father and the Father in me: or else believe me for the very works' sake." John xiv. 8–11. It is very plain that Jesus did not mean that he was the very Father himself, but that he represented him; so that to see him was to see the Father. The Invisible is thus said to be seen in his representative. The Son of man was the representative of the invisible God, for "in him dwelt all the fullness of the Godhead bodily."

Fourth. The Scriptures teach that by him God made, upholds and governs all things. Paul, in Eph. iii. 9, says that "God created all things by Jesus Christ;" and in Col. i. 16, 17, "For by him were all things created that are in heaven and that are in earth, visible and invisible, whether they be thrones or dominions or principalities or powers; all things were created by him and for him; and he is before all things, and by him all things consist." And in Heb. i. 2, he says, that "by him God made the worlds;" or constituted the ages or dispensations of Divine Providence and grace. When, therefore, Jesus said to the Jews, "My Father worketh hitherto and I work," he identified himself with God in all his works. The Jews then sought to kill him for thus seeming to make himself equal with God; but Jesus answered, "Verily, verily, I say unto you, the Son can do nothing of himself, but what he seeth the Father do; for what things soever he doth, those also doth the Son likewise." John v. 17, 19. And again: "For as the Father hath life in himself, so hath he given to the Son to have life in himself; and hath given him authority to execute judgment also, because he is the Son of Man." John v. 26, 27. Here Jesus disclaimed any and all independent action or operation. He did nothing of himself, and could do nothing of himself, but he was the medium of all the Father's operations in creating, upholding, and judging or governing the world.

Fifth. The Scriptures teach that he came into the world by incarnation, obeyed the law, suffered for sin, died on the cross, arose from the dead, and ascended into heaven, that he might effect and carry on the work of human redemption. Jesus said to the Jews, John vi. 33, "For the bread of God is HE which cometh down from heaven, and giveth life unto the world." And, (v. 38,) "For I came down from heaven, not to do my own will, but the will of him that sent me." The Jews murmured at him because he said, "I am the bread which came down from heaven." And they said, "Is not this Jesus, the son of Joseph, whose father and mother we know? how is it then that he saith, I came down from heaven?"

Jesus then justified his saying, that He was the bread of life, and added, (v. 51,) "I am the living bread which came down from heaven; if a man eat of this bread he shall live forever; and the bread that I will give is my flesh, which I will give for the life of the world." But, without quoting the whole passage, it is to be observed from what I have quoted, as well as the entire argument in connection, that Jesus intended that they should understand that HE, the very and identical Son of man, came down from heaven; and not that he had reference to any such hypothesis as that he had two natures or persons, one of which was heavenly and divine, and the other earthly and human. For he asserted that the bread which came down from heaven was his flesh which he would give for the life of the world. And when many of his disciples murmured, saying, "This is a hard saying; who can hear it?" Jesus said to them, (vv. 61. 62,) "Doth this offend you? What and if you shall see the Son of man ascend up where he was before?" Implying that he the Son of man had existed in heaven, and had really come down from heaven, and should ascend into heaven again. Hence Paul says, "He that ascended, what is it but that he also descended first into the lower parts of the earth." Now it was Jesus the Son of man who ascended, it was therefore Jesus the Son of man who descended first into the lower parts of the earth, *i. e.* became incarnated and suffered and died. With this agree these declarations of Jesus, John xvi. 28, "I came forth from the Father, and am come into the world: again I leave the world and go to the Father;" and Matt. xx. 28, "For the Son of man is not come to be ministered unto, but to minister, and to give his life a ransom for many." And it is written, John i. 14, " And the Word was made flesh and dwelt among us (and we beheld his glory, the glory as of the only begotten of the Father), full of grace and truth." The Word was made flesh, accords with Christ's own representation that his flesh is the bread of life which came down from heaven, and that we can have eternal life only by believing in the incarnate Word. Paul, speaking of this great mystery, says, Tim. iii. 16, "God was manifest in the flesh, justified in the Spirit, seen of angels, preached unto the gentiles, believed on in the world, received up into glory." And Heb. ii. 9, "But we see Jesus, who was made a little lower than the angels for the suffering of death, crowned with glory and honor." Again, Rom. i. 3, 4, "Jesus Christ our Lord was made of the seed of David according to the flesh, and declared to be the Son of God with power, according to the Spirit of holiness, by the resurrection from the dead." And again, Phil. ii. 6-8, " Who, being in the form of God, thought it no robbery to be as God; but made himself of no reputation, and took upon him the form of a servant, and was made in the likeness of men; and being found in fashion as a man, he humbled himself and became obedient unto death, even the death of the cross." It is impossible to make these passages agree with either the humanitarian scheme, or the semi-humanitarian; for they distinctly show that he who came into the world by incarnation, obeyed, suffered, died on the cross and rose again, was the Son and representative of God, who had previously been in the form of

God and, in that pre-existent state, thought it no robbery to appear as God.

Sixth. The Scriptures teach that he is the same person through all dispensations and in all forms or conditions. Paul says, Heb. xiii. 8, that "Jesus Christ (is) the same yesterday and to-day, and forever." He is the same who was with God in the beginning, and by whom all things were made—the same who being in the form of God, the representative of God, appeared as God in all the theophanies of the Old Testament times—the same who, becoming incarnate, took on him the form of a servant and manifested God in the flesh—the same who now dwells in the unapproachable light of the holiest of all in the heavens—the same who will come again the second time in the glory of the Father. John says, "That which was from the beginning, which we have heard, which we have seen with our eyes, which we have looked upon, and our hands have handled of the word of life, (for the life was manifested, and we have seen it, and bear witness, and show unto you that eternal life which was with the Father, and was manifested unto us,) that which we have seen and heard, declare we unto you, that ye also may have fellowship with us; and truly our fellowship is with the Father and with his Son Jesus Christ." 1 John i. 1–3. From this passage we learn that he who was heard, and seen and handled by the apostles, was the same person who was in the beginning with God. It was the man Christ Jesus whom they heard, and looked upon and handled, and the same was with the Father in the beginning. It was the Word that was in the beginning with God. It was the Word made flesh, whom they heard, saw and handled. The Jehovah of the Old Testament is the Jesus of the New. Before the incarnation he appeared in the form of God, afterward in the form of a servant. He who appeared to Isaiah on a throne high and lifted up, and whose train filled the temple, is the same who took a towel and girded himself and washed his disciples' feet. And in Heb. i. 6-12, Paul says: "When again he bringeth in the first-begotten into the world, he saith, And let all the angels of God worship him. And of the angels he saith, Who maketh his angels spirits, and his ministers a flame of fire. But unto the Son he saith, Thy throne, O God, is forever and ever; a sceptre of righteousness is the sceptre of thy kingdom: thou hast loved righteousness and hated iniquity: therefore God, even thy God, hath anointed thee with the oil of gladness above thy fellows. And, Thou, Lord, in the beginning hast laid the foundation of the earth; and the heavens are the works of thy hands; they shall perish, but thou remainest; and they shall all wax old, as doth a garment; and as a vesture shalt thou fold them up, and they shall be changed: but thou art the same and thy years shall not fail." The Psalms xcvii., xlv. and cii., from which the apostle quotes, all relate to the second advent of Christ, when again the Father shall bring his only begotten into the world, and give to him the throne of his father David, and establish his kingdom forever, and when the saints are to be joint or fellow-heirs with him; though he will be anointed with the oil of gladness above them. It was by him the Father created all things, and while, for the redemption of man, it has been found necessary to change the physical heavens and earth by a flood, and will be found necessary to change them again by fire, the Son of God, the one Mediator, remains the same through all changes, and his years shall not fail; neither shall he faint nor be discouraged till he shall have set judgment in the earth, and the isles shall wait for his law. The heavens and earth that are now, like the heavens and earth which were before the flood, must be changed and pass away, and give place to the new heavens and new earth wherein dwelleth righteousness; but he remains the same. The same Jesus who ascended from Olivet shall come again, and he who was crowned with the acanthus and mocked by the soldiers, will then wear the diadem of universal sovereignty, and all things shall be subdued to his sway. He is the same yesterday, and to-day and forever.

> " As much when in the manger laid
> Almighty ruler of the sky,
> As when the six days' work he made,
> Filled all the morning stars with joy."

Seventh. The scriptures teach that he is LORD of all. At his birth the angels said to the shepherds, "Unto you is born this day, in the city of David, a Saviour which is Christ the Lord." Luke ii. 11. David called him Lord, saying "The LORD said unto my Lord, sit at my right hand, until I make thy foes thy footstool." "Therefore," says Peter, "Let all the house of Israel know that God hath made that same Jesus whom ye crucified, both Lord and Christ." Acts ii. 34–36. "Jesus Christ is Lord of all." Acts x. 36. "Wherefore God hath highly exalted him, and given him a name which is above every name; that at the name of Jesus every knee should bow, of those in heaven, and those in earth, and those under the earth, and that every tongue should confess that Jesus Christ is Lord to the glory of God the Father." Phil. ii. 9–11. "The second man is the Lord from heaven." 1 Cor. xv. 47. From these passages and their connection, as well as other scriptures, we learn that he who was born of the Virgin, who was made in the likeness of men, who was crucified, who rose from the dead, ascended into heaven, sat down at the right hand of the Majesty on high, and shall come again at the last day, is Lord of all. And there is no other Lord but Jesus Christ, as there is no other God but the Father: "For though there be that are called gods, whether in heaven or in earth (as there be Gods many and Lords many;) But to us there is but one God, the Father, of whom are all things, and we in him; and one Lord Jesus Christ, by whom are all things, and we by him." 1 Cor. viii. 5, 6.

The Son of man is Lord also of the sabbath. He is the Christ the Son of the living God; who dwelt in the bosom of the Father, before the world was, and by whom God constituted the ages or dispensations. He was then the Lord of the sabbath at its original institution; for as God created all things by Jesus Christ, it was he of whom it is predicated, "For in six days the Lord made heaven and earth, and on the seventh day he rested and was refreshed," Exod. xxxi. 17, language which could not apply to the self-existent and unchangeable God, who fainteth not neither is weary. But Jesus Christ, as the representative of God, and by whom he made all things, and in whom God may be said to have rested on the seventh day, rested then from the work of creation, and sanctified the sabbath as creation's holyday, and gave it to man in his primitive state of innocence as a day of rest from labor—a day of religious service—a day of spiritual improvement—a day of glorious anticipation of perfect blessedness. The Lord Jesus made man, and he made the sabbath for man. The day and its use were designated by him, and he has the absolute control of it. He is Lord of the sabbath.

After the fall of man, when it became necessary that the Son of God should, in some period of the work of redemption, assume a conditional affinity to our race, indicated by the declaration that the seed of the woman should bruise the serpent's head, he was still, as before, the Lord of the sabbath, and in perpetuating the institution, as redemption's working-day, had the right to determine the time and manner of its observance under all the dispensations of grace, as well as the authority to enjoin it upon all the children of Adam.

The Son of man was therefore Lord of the sabbath before the law, and it was, doubtless, by his commandment appropriated to a religious use. It is said that at the END OF DAYS Cain and Abel brought their offerings to the Lord. No other time could be appropriately termed the *end of days* but the sabbath, which being the seventh was the end of the week. Sacrifices were no doubt required to be offered on that day in the worship of God, and Abel brought of the firstlings of his flock and of the fat thereof, thus showing his faith in the great sin-offering of which this sacrifice was a type. Cain's offering showed his want of faith. Sacrifices continued to be offered by the faithful through the antediluvian age, and the first thing done by Noah after the flood was to offer sacrifice to God. These sacrifices were then, as well as subsequently, without doubt, associated with times and seasons. And Melchisedek, the priest of the most High God, and Abraham, Isaac and Jacob, and their posterity, must have known the Divine appointment of the seventh day, and observed it accordingly. We have indeed no specific account of its observance; but we must not thence infer that it was not observed; for the Son of man who said, " Before Abraham was I am," and "Abraham rejoiced to see MY DAY, and he saw it and was glad," was then the Lord of the Sabbath which was a type of that Day of the Lord to which Abraham also by faith looked forward. Christ's day has been from the beginning set forth by its appropriate symbol, weekly recurring to cheer the heirs of promise. And in the observance of the sabbath they have expressed their faith, walked with God, and become heirs of eternal life.

The Son of man was Lord of the Sabbath under the Law. It was he who was with the congregation in the wilderness. He made the Sabbath the sign of the national covenant between them and himself, and commanded it to be kept as a test of their obedience —a ground of their justification and a means of their sanctification. He it was who from Sinai spake the word of the law, and said "Remember the sabbath day to keep it holy." He gave to Moses all the special enactments concerning its observance as the sign of their covenant. He renewed his covenant with them in all their generations, sending his prophets to them, rising up early and sending them, but they would not hear. And at last he came himself in the flesh, made of a woman, made under the law, and obeyed the law; but they despised him and rejected him. And the sabbath, as a sign of their national covenant, was abrogated when he lay in the sepulchre, the crucified one. In breaking that covenant, in all their generations, they made it manifest that no nation in natural flesh could be trained for the kingdom of God, or prepared for the enjoyment of the glory and blessedness of the millennial sabbath. Hence the natural seed were as a nation rejected—their covenant abolished, and its sign, so far as respected that specific day, in its aspect to the nation, abrogated. The Jewish people are now without a sabbath. The Lord of the sabbath having abrogated the sign, and their house is left unto them desolate.

The Son of man is Lord also of the sabbath under the Gospel. In the end of the Jewish sabbath, as it began to dawn on the first day of the week, he rose from the dead, introducing a new order of things, and consecrating that day as the time of the observance of religious worship during the new dispensation of grace to man. It was indeed the end of the Jewish sabbath, terminating with it the hope of the natural seed by the abrogation of the sign of the national covenant. It was the beginning of the sabbath of a new dispensation in which we are begotten again unto a lively hope by the resurrection of our Lord Jesus Christ from the dead. The use of the sabbath as a sign of a national covenant and test of obedience, ended when the trial of the natural seed ended. The Lord of the sabbath has therefore dispensed with the observance of the seventh day because of its special appropriation under the law, as the sign of the national covenant, now abrogated, and its legal use as a test of obedience. There is now no national covenant under the Gospel. The Gospel is not a national system for the trial of any nation in natural flesh. All nations were tried in Israel as the representative nation, and all have been rejected in Israel. And the natural Jew is, wherever found in all the world, a living testimony that by the deeds of the law no flesh living can be justified. The Gospel is, on the other hand, a system of universal grace to be preached among all nations for the obedience of faith, and the sanctification of all believers, who, with the saints of former ages, shall constitute the seed of faith—a holy nation—a royal priesthood—a peculiar people, and be heirs of the promised inheritance.

In designating the first day of the week as the sabbath under the Gospel, the Lord of the sabbath has not made it the sign of the covenant with the seed of faith, nor made it the special test of obedience: for he has not required the observance of days with their special religious institutions as the condition of justification. The seed of faith have in all ages been justified by faith and not by the deeds of the law. Hence the observance of the sabbath is nowhere enjoined as a condition of justification before the law, nor under the Gospel; and only required as such nationally under the law, for the purpose of showing that no flesh living could be justified by the law. And none of Israel were justified during their national trial; but those who believed, and who served in the newness of the spirit and not in the oldness of the letter. But the obligations to observe the sabbath under the Gospel are not weakened. Faith does not make void the law of God: it establishes the law. The believer is furnished with a motive power and a spiritual energy by which he is enabled to keep the law, and so walk worthy of the vocation wherewith he is called. The first day of the week is rendered sacred to him by the resurrection of Christ, and has all the sanction of the authority of Christ for its observance as the sabbath. The Lord of the sabbath has placed its due observance among the moral obligations of all to whom the Gospel is preached. The Gospel knows no other sabbath but it, and no other Lord of the sabbath but the Son of man.

The Son of man is Lord of the Millennial sabbath. Paul says, "For unto the angels hath he not put in subjection the world to come of which we speak; but one in a certain place testified, saying, "What is man that thou art mindful of him; and the Son of man that thou visitest him. Thou madest him a little lower than the angels: thou crownedst him with glory and honor, and didst set him over the work of thy hands: Thou hast put all things in subjection under his feet. For in that he put all in subjection under him, he left nothing that is not put under him. But now we see not all things put under him. But we see Jesus, who was made a little lower than the angels for the sufferings of death, crowned with glory and honor; that he, by the grace of God, should taste death for every man. Heb. ii. 5–9. The honor and dignity with which the first representative man was created and the dominion given to him, is here considered as having been transferred to the second representative man, under whom, however, we see not yet all things subjected. But in the world to come, that is in the Millennium, the great Day of the Lord, all things shall be put under him. Then shall he, who was made a little lower than the angels for the suffering of death, be exalted in glory, and reign over all the earth. Then shall the second Adam take the dominion forfeited by the first Adam. Then shall the Church of God, the second Eve, be exalted with Christ, and made partaker of his glory. To the Divine Adam and his redeemed and glorified consort will all things be put in subjection; and every knee shall bow to him, and every tongue confess that he is Lord to the glory of God the Father.

Isaiah, in the second chapter of his prophecy, speaking of that period when the Lord's house shall be established in the top of the mountains, and exalted above the hills, and all nations shall flow unto it; when he shall judge among the nations, and the subjects of his government shall beat their swords into plowshares and their spears into pruning-hooks, (says v. 11,) that "the Lord alone shall be exalted in that day." And Zechariah says, "Then the Lord shall be king over all the earth; there shall be one Lord and his name one." Zech. xiv. 9. Then the kingdoms of this world shall become the kingdom of our Lord and Saviour Jesus Christ, and he shall reign in Mount Zion and in Jerusalem, and before his ancients gloriously.

> "Come, then, and added to thy many crowns,
> Receive yet one, the crown of all the earth,
> Thou who alone art worthy! It was thine
> By ancient covenant, ere Nature's birth;
> And thou hast made it thine by purchase since,
> And overpaid its value with thy blood.
> Thy saints proclaim thee king; and in their hearts
> Thy title is engraven with a pen
> Dipped in the fountain of eternal love.
> *　　*　　*　　*　　*　　*　　*
> Come, then, and added to thy many crowns,
> Receive yet one, as radiant as the rest,
> Due to thy last and most effectual work,
> Thy word fulfilled, the conquest of a world."

CHAPTER V.

THE OBSERVANCE OF THE SABBATH.

"And he said unto them, The sabbath was made for man, and not man for the sabbath. Therefore the Son of man is Lord also of the sabbath."—Mark ii. 27, 28.

IN regard to the observance of the sabbath we have to guard against two fatal errors: the one, that of subjecting man to the sabbath, so as to make him the driveling slave of an arbitrary institution, and thus sacrificing human welfare to its sanctification: the other, that of subjecting the sabbath to man, so as to allow him to appropriate it to whatever use he pleases without regard to its sanctification. Man was not made for the sabbath: his comfort and happiness are not of secondary importance to the sanctification of the day. The sabbath is not an *end* to be placed above the necessities of humanity; but a *means* designed for the spiritual benefit of mankind. Such an observance of the sabbath as shrouds its atmosphere with gloom, and renders its services irksome and oppressive; which clothes the soul with a starched and unbending austerity; which encases the spirit in an icy formality; which oppresses the conscience with numberless rigid exactions; which restrains every gladsome emotion of the mind by a wearisome scrupulousness; which despoils the heart of every natural joy, and renders religion itself an intolerable burden, is a burlesque upon the institution, and a mere bugbear to children. The soul in such a thraldom finds nothing joyous or elevating in private devotion, family worship, or church ordinances. The whole affair becomes a tiresome drudgery, in which the unwilling Pharisee forces himself to dole out with scrupulous exactness the sanctimonious services whereby he expects to purchase a seat in the kingdom of heaven. It were better that the sabbath should be dispensed with altogether, than that such a slavish burden should be imposed upon the people of God. A more unsightly appendage to the Gospel of Christ could scarcely be conceived; and yet there are some who seem to have no higher conception of the sabbath than this, and who make it a grievous burden, by the demureness of constraint imposed in a strictly legal observance of the day.

On the other hand, that the sabbath was made for man, must not be construed so as to sanction a desecration of the day, and allow every one to do whatever he pleases in appropriating its sacred hours to indolence, business or pleasure. The sabbath is not to be subject to man's whim or caprice. It is not left to his option whether he shall keep it or not: the command is, "Remember the sabbath day to keep it holy." He is forbidden to work or play—to seek his carnal pleasure or his worldly gain. It is not a matter of indifference whether it be kept holy, or spent in utter disregard to its sanctification. The sabbath is an institution—a divine institution—and was made for man's use according to its nature and design, and not for his abuse according to his own will or inclination. The sabbath was made for man's spiritual improvement, and this required that he should cease from business and labor. It was made for man's spiritual improvement, hence it must not be spent in listless indolence or in pursuit of carnal pleasures. To lounge about home, or rove through the streets and fields, or make railroad or steamboat excursions, or take a drive into the country, for amusement and recreation, is an abuse of the sabbath. By these and similar means of pleasure-seeking, some diversion of mind from the ordinary business and cares of life may be obtained, but no true refreshment to the soul is found, and the end and design of the institution is lost.

The sabbath was made for man—for his spiritual benefit. In his original state of innocency it was designed to furnish him with leisure from worldly and secular concerns, for intellectual and moral improvement; and had he not sinned it would, doubtless, have been employed in purely spiritual exercises to that end, as there would then have been no occasion for the diversion of any part of its sacred time to other purposes. What the first Eden sabbath was to man, it would have continued to be, until all should have been perfected in holiness, established in virtue, and exalted to the enjoyment of an endless rest—a sabbath of unceasing pleasure in the presence of God. And a Millennium of glory would have crowned the obedience of man with an everlasting reward.

The fall of man by sin, rendered necessary a change in his condition so as to ensure the execution of the penalty of transgression; and man was expelled from the Garden of Eden, and debarred from the tree of life, that having no access to it as the appointed means of health, he should, through disease and the decline of his natural powers, be brought down to death within a thousand years, which with the Lord is as one day, and was indicated in the words, "In the day thou eatest thereof thou shalt surely die." The deterioration of the physical condition of man was then, however, no greater than was necessary to effect the execution of the penalty, and his circumstances were such that the least possible interference with the regular observance of the sabbath could occur. It was possible for man, in the antediluvian age, to have observed the sabbath in almost its Eden perfection. Still, occasions doubtless arose when, for works of mercy and necessity, the rest of the sabbath might have been innocently broken.

But, further, when it had been demonstrated, by the actual results of the ante-diluvian age, that the physical condition of the world was too good for man's moral benefit, another change was required to adapt it to the purposes of redemption. Man needed a severer discipline, and by the deluge such a change was effected as was demanded. The life of man was shortened; he was made subject to vanity, and his circumstances became such as frequently to render it necessary to violate the rest of the sabbath, or sacrifice his comfort and well-being. The example and teachings of Christ, the Lord of the sabbath, have a special bearing upon this point.

On one occasion, as Jesus passed through the fields

on the sabbath day, his disciples, being hungry, began to pluck the ears of corn, and to eat the grain, which they shelled by rubbing them in their hands. Against this the Pharisees demurred as a violation of the sabbath. But Jesus justified his disciples by reference to the case of David and his men, who, when hungry, went into the house of God and ate of the shew-bread which the priest only might do lawfully. Their necessity, at the time, justified the common use of the sanctified bread; and so human necessity justifies the common use of a holy day. A work of necessity may be performed on the sabbath. Man may have need of food or medicine, or medical attendance and nursing—indeed, he may be subject to various necessities, coming on him in the order of nature and providence, which may be supplied on the sabbath day as far as he may have means and opportunity of doing so, although in so doing he may be obliged to violate the sanctity thereof.

Again, Jesus said to them, "Have ye not read in the law, how that on the sabbath days, the priests in the temple profane the sabbath, and are blameless? But I say unto you, that in this place is one greater than the temple." To profane the sabbath was to work on the sabbath. Now in man's primitive condition the services of religion consisted in only devout meditation and grateful praise, and sweet and holy communing with God. There were no sacrificial offerings needed, and no ritual observances of a laborious character; but since the fall of man, the services of religion have been adapted to the great purpose of redemption, and in all ages of the world the ministers of religion have had sacrifices to offer, or other services to perform requiring more or less labor, hence they have been obliged, in the discharge of their functions, to violate the rest of the sabbath. And such violation is pronounced blameless by the Lord of the sabbath, who, in the economy of his mercy, has constituted the sabbath redemption's working-day. The religious character of the services performed by the priests in the temple justified their profanation of the day. Their work was essential to the end for which the day was made and the temple was built. But Jesus, the Son of God himself, the Lord of the sabbath, being greater than the temple, was there, and by his example and teaching justified all works of benevolence and mercy in the service of humanity. This doctrine of Christ especially justified all labor or work necessarily associated with the services of religion. Religious works may be performed on the sabbath day. These works are designed to promote man's spiritual improvement, and hence accord with the design of the institution. Under the economy of redemption they are necessary to a profitable keeping of the sabbath. In this category, we may also place the work of sabbath-school teaching, which, properly conducted, is a religious work, calculated greatly to promote the spiritual improvement of the young, and implant in their minds the seed of faith.

Again, Jesus said unto them, "If ye had known what this meaneth, I will have mercy and not sacrifice, ye would not have condemned the guiltless. For the Son of man is Lord also of the sabbath day." Paul says that man was " made subject to vanity," to a severe providential discipline, which has aggravated his helplessness and misery and shortened his days, "not willingly," not arbitrarily or unnecessarily, "but by reason of him who hath subjected the same in hope;" it being a means adopted in divine wisdom for the redemption of man. In like manner, sacrifices and offerings were ordained of God, not because he had any pleasure in them, but as a provision of mercy for human salvation. And so the sabbath was instituted, not for the sake of the day itself, but for man's benefit, to secure him time for the advancement of his spiritual interests. And as man's salvation is the end and design of all these institutions, they are to be strictly observed in accordance with that end, as far as practicable; but when their observance would require a sacrifice of human welfare, or interfere with the preservation of life and property, it may be dispensed with. The necessities of mankind are paramount to all ceremonial institutions, sacrificial rites and holy days. The Priest and Levite who passed by the half-murdered man on the road from Jerusalem to Jericho, without rendering him assistance lest they should be ceremonially defiled, were recreant to the claims of humanity and violated the higher law, "Thou shalt love thy neighbor as thyself." A Jew, in London, many years ago, having fallen into a sewer on the seventh day, refused to be lifted out because it was his sabbath. This being reported to the king, his majesty ordered that, since the Jew would not be lifted out on the seventh day, lest he should break his sabbath, he should not be lifted out on the first day, but should be compelled to observe the Christian sabbath in like manner: or that none should break the Christian sabbath by lifting him out. Before Monday morning, however, the Jew died from hunger and exposure in so foul a place. In this case, while we pity the poor Jew on account of his superstition, we cannot but censure the king on account of his inhumanity. Both were wrong; but the king's wrong was the worst. God says, "I will have mercy and not sacrifice." And Jesus Christ, the Son of God, took our condition, and learned by actual subjection to our infirmities and trials, the necessities and sorrows of our fallen state, that he might know how to sympathize with us in our weakness and wo; and, as the Lord of the sabbath, he says, in this connection, "I will have mercy and not sacrifice." He has therefore adapted the sabbath to the condition of man, that its observance should not be a grievous bondage, a slavish and oppressive tyranny; but that it should be a delightful antepast of an eternal rest of love and joy.

In accordance with this saying, "I will have mercy and not sacrifice," Jesus performed many of his wondrous cures on the sabbath day. A man with a withered hand had gone to the synagogue to worship on the sabbath. Jesus met him there. The Jews watched to see whether he would heal him. Perhaps they thought that he would do so secretly. But Jesus said to the man, "Stand forth." Then, calling their attention to his case, he asked, " Whether is it lawful to do good on the sabbath day or to do evil? to save life or to kill?" But they were silent. And he said to them, "What man shall there be among you that shall have a sheep, and if it fall into a pit on the sabbath day, will he not lay hold on it, and lift it out? How much better then is a man than a sheep? Wherefore it is lawful to do well on the sabbath day." And he said to the man, "Stretch forth thy hand." And he did so, and it was immediately healed. In this and other cases we find that whatever work was requisite to effect the cure, or properly manifest it to the glory of God, and whatever was suitable for the relief and comfort of the afflicted person, was done. Hence he commanded the impotent man who lay at the pool of Bethesda to rise, take up his bed and go to his house: and, anointing the eyes of the blind man with spittle and clay, he sent him to the pool of Siloam to wash.

And Jesus, when he healed the woman who had an infirmity eighteen years, rebuked the opposition of the ruler of the synagogue, saying, "Thou hypocrite, doth not each one of you, on the sabbath, loose his ox or his ass from the stall and lead him away to watering? And ought not this woman, being a daughter of Abraham, whom Satan hath bound, lo, these eighteen years be loosed from this bond on the sabbath day?"

Thus are we taught that works of necessity and mercy are lawful on the sabbath day. Hence, when life or property is in danger, the necessary steps may be taken to save them. Means may be employed for the removal of disease and the restoration of health. Needful food may be prepared, provided the necessity is not the result of intentional neglect or design. The sick may be visited, and friendly visits for religious

THE OBSERVANCE OF THE SABBATH. 125

discourse and edification may be paid; but they should be so timed as not to interfere with or prevent attention to other important duties.

Let no one take advantage of this saying, "I will have mercy and not sacrifice," to justify willful and needless profanations of the sabbath. The end or design of the sabbath must be kept in view, and it should be religiously observed in accordance therewith, except when the demand of necessity or mercy require a departure therefrom. It will be well to remember that the eye of the Lord is upon us at all times, and that he knows whether there is a real necessity or not for the work that is done on the sabbath. Men may deceive themselves, and offer plausible excuses to others for their needless profanation of the sabbath: but they cannot deceive God, and only involve themselves in guilt and ruin. A chemist and druggist once remarked to an American author, "There was a time when I used to court business on the Lord's day; and sheltering myself under the alleged necessity of being on hand to supply medicines in case of illness, I employed myself in preparing tinctures, soda powders, etc., for the sake of saving time on other days. At that time I took more money on the sabbath than on any other day, not a penny in a shilling of which was for matters of real necessity. When I began to see it to be my duty to act differently, and refused to sell perfumery, cigars, etc., on the sabbath, I offended a few, and expected to find my business would be seriously injured. But it turned out otherwise. I now enjoy my sabbaths, and can say with humble thankfulness that my prosperity is greater than ever."

A distinguished physician, finding his calls to be so many on the sabbath as to make it impossible for him to attend to public worship, made it known that he would not make any charge for Sunday visits, in the hope that out of delicacy but few would send for him. But he found himself overrun on that day; for everybody could afford to be sick and need a physician on Sunday. He then altered his plan, and gave notice that he would charge double for Sunday visits. After that he was seldom sent for on the sabbath, and then only in extreme cases; so that he could afterward enjoy his sabbaths by a regular attendance on religious service.

There are doubtless cases of disease in which the services of a physician are required on the sabbath, and they should be attended to without making double charge; but ordinarily these might be so arranged as not materially to interfere with the due observance of the day. And in like manner apothecaries might so arrange their hours for compounding medicines for the sick, that they could avail themselves of the privilege of attending the public worship of God. There is certainly no necessity that they should keep open for the sale of cigars, mineral water, etc. The sin of sabbath-breaking is sadly increasing. Look at our cities. See the thousands of taverns and grog-shops, either boldly thrown open for the sale of intoxicating drinks, or with fronts closed and side-doors open, dealing out stealthily the drunkard's poison. Cigar and tobacco stores, confectionaries and beer-shops, are many of them engaged in vending their different commodities on the sabbath. Bakers and barbers generally carry on their business as usual. Stage, steamboat and railroad companies endeavor to profit by getting up excursions or running their lines on the Lord's day. And whatever excuses may be offered for these things, it is evident that the great aim is to make money. If it were found that these violations of the sabbath were attended with pecuniary loss, horses would have leave to rest in their stalls, steamboats would lie at the wharf, and the steam-engine would sleep in the depot. If men could make money by going to church, it would no longer be convenient to remain at home. Mankind generally seem to think more of money than they do of virtue or of God himself. They look at the things which are seen and not at the unseen. Temporal interests and sensual pleasures engage their thoughts and eternal things are banished from their minds. Present advanges blind their eyes to future consequences, and eternal salvation is risked, is, indeed, bartered away for the increased profits supposed to accrue from pursuing their business on the sabbath.

But it may be questioned whether, in the long-run, it is not a losing business, even in this world, to work on the sabbath. Seven young men, in a town in Massachusetts, started in the same business nearly at the same time. Six of them had some property or assistance from their friends, and followed their business on the sabbath, as well as on the other six days. The other had less property than either of the six. He had less assistance from friends, and worked only six days, keeping the sabbath holy. In a few years he was the only one of the seven who had any property and had not failed in business.

"I have particularly observed," says a respectable merchant of New York, "that those who kept their counting-rooms open on the sabbath during my residence there of twenty-five years, have failed without exception." Another gentleman says, "I can recollect more than fifty years; but I cannot recollect a case of a man in the town where I reside, who was accustomed to work on the sabbath, who did not fail or lose his property before he died."

Sir Matthew Hale was very strict in observing the sabbath, and he tells us that he had found by experience that any attention given to his clients or their business on the Lord's day, did never further his cause any; but rather tended to injure it. And he therefore peremptorily refused to attend to any business on the sabbath, though he had as much business on hand as any other man in England, both before and after he was made judge.

Examples of this kind are numerous enough to show that God, by his special providence, has sanctioned the observance of the Lord's day, and placed the stamp of condemnation upon the willful desecration of it. But in their mad pursuit after wealth and pleasure, men are as deaf to the voice of God in providence as they are to his voice in revelation. Nothing restrains them from the most flagrant violations of the sabbath, but the penalties annexed to its desecration by the civil law. And they are loudly urging their petitions to have those penalties removed so far as may be necessary for them to profit by the sabbath as a common holyday. These spiders of the community are very willing that the flies may all be out, so that they may only be allowed to spread their nets to catch them. They would have all factories and workshops closed, that the unoccupied operatives may be enticed to spend their hard-earned money in dissipation and pleasure-seeking. And thousands have no more wit than to suppose that these caterers to a carnal appetite, these tempters from the right ways of the Lord, are their benefactors and friends, and join with them in petitioning legislatures and councils to allow them to make game of them in their violation of the sabbath.

We are generally more apt to be lax in our observance of the sabbath than overstrict in keeping it. Could we give the sabbath a tongue, what complaints might it not make against its very friends? Alas! would it not say, "To what indignities am I not subjected? Many will sit up on Saturday night, and work or keep their shops open till midnight, because they can make up their lack of sleep by lying abed so much later in the morning, thus wasting my precious hours in slumber. And then they don't go to church because they can't get ready in time. The afternoon is spent in visiting their friends or receiving calls, and they won't go to church at night, because they want to rise early on Monday morning, and therefore they must go to bed in season. The languge of their conduct, if not their words, is, "When will the sabbath be gone, that we may buy and sell and get gain?" We might enlarge upon this point, and show the numerous ways in which the sabbath is desecrated by its professed friends. But space will not permit. The neglect of the means of grace, the disregard of the sanctuary, the contempt of religious ordinances, manifested in the indolent lounging about home, the secular employment, the vain and trifling conversation of professors of religion, show that there is a sad deficiency of the spirit of Christ, and a dangerous conformity to the world. Professors of religion who violate the sabbath unnecessarily in seeking their own pleasure and ease, little think of the pernicious influence of their example. Men of the world watch for the failings of professors of religion, sneer at their inconsistencies, denounce their hypocrisy, and justify themselves in an open disregard of the sabbath and religious institutions by their faults.

A suitable preparation should be made previous to the sabbath, that it may be kept holy. "Six days shalt thou labor and do all thy work." All business necessary to be attended to before Monday morning should be transacted by Saturday evening. The week's work should all be done, that none of its cares be carried over into the sabbath day. If a person has so much to do that he cannot accomplish it all in six days, he should either procure some one to assist him, or else curtail his business. He has no right to steal the hours of the sabbath for secular employment. Posting books, making out bills, writing business letters, and other ways in which tradesmen and others frequently employ a portion of the sabbath, is altogether wrong and pernicious in its influence upon the mind. Any other kind of work might as well be done. The command requires that all the work—

all the secular business of the week, shall be done in six days. On the sabbath thou shalt not do any work, neither employ any one to work for you in your secular business on that day.

In the house also every suitable preparation should be made in providing food, fuel and clothing, that the spiritual exercises of the family, their attendance at church, and their profit from the means of grace, may be interfered with as little as possible. It is a bad sign to see professors of religion going to the barber's and the baker's on the sabbath morning. It is a bad sign if the tailor, mantua-maker, milliner, hatter or shoemaker to send their work home on the sabbath morning. There are many little things which might be attended to on the previous day, that are negligently suffered by most professors to pass over undone until sabbath morning, and then all are in haste to have their little chores done in time for church. How much better if all preparations were made on Saturday, and that there should be nothing to draw off the thoughts from the contemplation of heavenly things on the Lord's day.

Every Christian especially should prepare, by private devotion and self-examination, for the profitable use of the means of grace, and a comfortable communion with God in the services of his house. And every one should be careful to be at the place of worship in due time, so as to be present at the beginning of the exercises; and not think himself in time if he only gets there soon enough to hear the text announced; as if the object were more to hear the preacher than to worship God. The hearing of faith is indeed of great importance; but they that have faith will exercise it toward God in devoutly preparing to profit by the word. And after a devout attendance on the services of God's house, let the intervening time be spent in accordance with the design of the day, in reading the Scriptures and religious books, meditation, prayer and praise, or in sabbath school teaching, visiting the sick, and other works of piety and mercy.

O! what a blessing would the sabbath prove if it were thus employed in cultivating the mind and heart and elevating the soul in communion with God. Then all dullness and wearisomeness would vanish. The sabbath would be called a delight and honorable. A holy cheerfulness would sweeten its passing hours—a divine elevation would gladden the spirit—a heavenly hope would fill the soul with rejoicing. A sabbath thus spent would form, as it was intended it should, the nearest approximation to the millennial sabbath that we may be now permitted to enjoy. It is the Millennium's symbol-day and should be its antepast. Then should we be made joyful through the blessed hope of that time which is emphatically called "the day of the Lord," that seventh millenary of the world, when all the saints of God shall be exalted with Christ in his glory. Isaiah celebrates that day, as from the hill of prophecy he viewed in the distance its coming glory. "And there shall come a rod out of the stem of Jesse, and a branch shall grow out of his roots. And the Spirit of the Lord shall rest upon him, the Spirit of wisdom and understanding, the Spirit of counsel and might, the Spirit of knowledge and of the fear of the Lord. And shall make him of quick understanding in the fear of the Lord; and he shall not judge after the sight of his eyes, neither reprove after the hearing of his ears. But with righteousness shall he judge the poor, and reprove with equity for the meek of the earth; and he shall smite the earth with the rod of his mouth, and with the breath of his lips shall he slay the wicked. And righteousness shall be the girdle of his loins, and faithfulness the girdle of his reins. The wolf also shall dwell with the lamb, and the leopard shall lie down with the kid; and the calf and the young lion and the fatling together, and a little child shall lead them. And the cow and the bear shall feed; their young ones shall lie down together, and the lion shall eat straw like the ox. And the sucking child shall play on the hole of the asp, and the weaned child shall put his hand on the cockatrice's den. They shall not hurt nor destroy in all my holy mountain; for the earth shall be full of the knowledge of the Lord as the waters cover the sea. And in that day there shall be a root of Jesse, which shall stand for an ensign of the people.' To it shall the gentiles seek, and his rest shall be glorious." Isa. xi. 1-10. The time here predicted is evidently the Millennium, or the good time coming, which has been the expectation of God's people for ages past; and the Rod and Branch of Jesse who shall reign in that time is Jesus Christ the Son of God, who was made of the seed of David the son of Jesse according to the flesh. The *Rest* is his—a consummation of his work during the six millenaries from man's fall unto the restitution of all things. The redemption of his elect church will then be completed, and as the bride, the Lamb's wife, she will enter with him into the enjoyment of that rest. Then shall the arm of the oppressor be broken, and rest be given to the nations, who shall beat their swords into plowshares and their spears into pruning-hooks and learn war no more. Every man shall sit under his own vine and fig-tree and none disturb his peace.

The sabbath was made for man; and for man will the Millennium sabbath dawn. The new heavens and earth, which according to his promise we look for, is promised to Christ and his saints, for therein shall all believers obtain a glorious and everlasting reward along with Christ in his kingdom. That promised glory and blessedness is not promised only to the people of God who may then be alive and remain on the earth, but to all the saints of God from Abel down to the coming of the Lord. For they who shall be alive and remain shall not hinder those who are asleep; but the dead in Christ shall rise and the living in Christ be changed at the same time and caught up to meet the Lord in the air, and all shall enter with him into the rest or sabbatism of glory and joy. But we must not suppose that the millennial sabbath will be to the saints a period of inert repose. Far from it. They will be made kings and priests unto God, and shall reign on the earth. They will be actively and delightfully employed in carrying on the administration of the heavenly kingdom, in governing the nations, in subduing and reconciling all the disobedient to the government of God. In this work they will find their highest satisfaction and enjoyment. A state of voluptuous indolence, such as many expect in heaven, would be a curse instead of a blessing to intelligent beings. The saints of God are to be a peculiar people, zealous of good works, and all the traits of Christian character here formed must come into active exercise in the future kingdom of Christ. The Millennial sabbath will be a perfect rest to them from all the work and trial of the present probationary life, and in the full enjoyment of the glory and blessedness promised as their reward.

Under their administration of the kingdom, the nations of the earth shall have rest. They shall pursue the arts of peace. War shall be known no more. Its horrid art shall be forgotten. Slavery shall cease. Its chains will be broken, and no more shall "man's inhumanity to man make countless millions mourn."

> "The groans of nature on this nether world,
> Which Heaven has heard for ages, have an end,
> Foretold by prophets, and by poets sung
> Whose fire was kindled at the prophet's lamp.
> The time of rest, the promised sabbath comes;
> Six thousand years of sorrow have well-nigh
> Fulfilled their tardy and disastrous course
> Over a sinful world; and what remains
> Of this tempestuous state of human things
> Is merely as the workings of a sea
> Before a calm, that rocks itself to rest.
> For he whose car the winds are, and the clouds
> The dust that waits upon his sultry march,
> When sin hath moved him, and his wrath is hot,
> Shall visit earth in mercy; shall descend

Propitious in his chariot paved with love ;
And what his storms have blasted and defaced
For man's revolt, shall with a smile repair."

Yes, we look and wait for that rest. We groan for that redemption, and hopefully anticipate the promised jubilee of earth. The nearer the Millennial sabbath approaches, the more carefully should we observe its hallowed symbol, and prepare for its glorious realities. If we have no taste for the religious services of the symbol-sabbath, how can we expect to enjoy the thing symbolized? Let us then assiduously cultivate a love for the sabbath and its holy duties, "not forsaking the assembling of ourselves together as the manner of some is; but exhorting one another, and so much the more as we see the day approaching." Hail, then, each sabbath morning with delight. Rise early that you may have the more time to spend in its appropriate religious exercises. Lift up your soul to God in devout contemplation—fervent prayer and grateful praise, and in your secret communing with heaven, let your soul be baptized with the Spirit, that you may be in the Spirit throughout the day. Gather your family together, and with them join in singing Jehovah's praise, reading his word, and offering the tribute of devotion. Take them to the house of God for public worship, and teach them to esteem the sabbath and its services as their greatest pleasure. And when the day of the Lord comes, God will bring you to his holy mountain and make you joyful in his house of prayer.

O happy day! Great sabbath of Redemption. Rest of the redeemed—of all the redeemed—of the redeemed from six thousand years of trial, toil and pain—of all who through faith have washed their robes and made them white in the blood of the Lamb. What glorious beauty shall thy peaceful years adorn! What substantial pleasures flow from the presence of the sabbath's Lord, and thrill with rapturous joy the glorified company! How exalted their condition! how heavenly! how divine! What magnificent developments will be made of the love of God to his chosen and sanctified ones! What a compensation for their work of labor and love which they have showed toward his name!

O day of the Lord! the seventh, in relation to the past, bringing sweet repose, and heavenly rest to the weary workers who shall compose the church of the saved; and yet the first in relation to the future, the embryo of a still more glorious and unending day of rest, when under the administration of the saints of God, with Jesus reigning, the subjection and reconciliation of all things shall have been effected, and all intelligences, in their appropriate conditions, shall bow the knee to Jesus, and confess him Lord, to the glory of God the Father; when the voices of earth shall all be tuned to a divine harmony, and join in the universal chorus of praise.

The purpose of God in relation to the nations of the earth, through the reign of the saints, will culminate at the end of a thousand years: and the Millennium sabbath will end, to be succeeded by other measures of the divine government toward the unrighteous dead who shall be raised from death and subjected and reconciled. But the condition of the saints will not end with the Millennium. They will be kings and priests unto God through all phases of the everlasting kingdom. Their rest of glory and blessedness shall never end; and when the grand consummation of the Divine purpose shall have been effected through their instrumentality, they will continue to REST in complete satisfation in God through all ages, world without end. The ultimate of the Divine purpose is A SABBATH FOR ALL, under the administration of the LORD OF THE SABBATH.

> "Too soon our earthly sabbath ends
> Cares of a work-day will return,
> And faint our hearts, and fitful burn:
> O think, my soul, beyond compare,
> Think what a sabbath must be there;
> Where all is holy bliss, that knows
> Nor imperfection, nor a close.

W Steel Sculp

THE DIVINE MAN.

A DIALOGUE

BETWEEN REASON AND REVELATION, ON THE INCORRUPTIBILITY OF THE SAVIOUR'S BODY.

REASON. Good-morning, Mr. Revelation, I am glad to meet with you. I have been desirous of consulting you on a question of great interest relating to the body of Christ.

REVELATION. I salute you in the Lord. Rom. xvi. 22. My doctrine is not mine, but his that sent me; if any man will do his will, he shall know of the doctrine, whether it be of God, or whether I speak of myself. John vii. 16, 17.

REA. The question is this — Was the body of Jesus Christ, the Son of David, liable to corruption or not?

REV. Let me freely speak unto you of the Patriarch David, that he is both dead and buried, and his sepulchre is with us unto this day. Therefore, being a prophet, and knowing that God had sworn with an oath to him, that of the fruit of his loins, according to the flesh, he would raise up Christ to sit on his throne; he seeing this before, spake of the resurrection of Christ, that his soul was not left in hell, neither did his flesh see corruption. Acts ii. 29–31.

REA. I believe the testimony that Christ rose from the dead, consequently was not left in the state of the dead, as was David; and so short was the period intervening between his death and resurrection, that he saw no putrefaction; but was this an essential quality of the body of Christ?

REV. And as concerning that he raised him from the dead, *now* no more to return to corruption, he said on this wise, I will give you the *sure mercies* of David. Wherefore he saith also in another Psalm, *Thou shalt not suffer thine holy one to see corruption.* For David, after he had served his own generation by the will of God, fell on sleep, and was laid unto his fathers, and saw corruption: but HE whom God raised again, SAW NO CORRUPTION. Acts xiii. 34–37.

REA. I am filled with comfort in the firm belief that Christ rose from the dead to die no more; and whether the body of Jesus was perishable or not, it was not the Divine will that any decomposition should take place in that body—therefore it saw no corruption; but would not that body have putrefied and decayed, had it remained *long enough* in the tomb?

REV. Him, being delivered by the determinate counsel and foreknowledge of God, ye have taken, and by wicked hands have crucified and slain; whom God raised up, having loosed the pains of death: *because it was* IMPOSSIBLE *that* HE *should be holden of it.* For David speaketh concerning him, I foresaw the Lord *always* before my face; for he is on my right hand, that I should not be moved: therefore did my heart rejoice, and my tongue was glad; *moreover also my* FLESH *shall* REST *in hope:* because *thou wilt not leave my soul in hell, neither wilt thou suffer thine* HOLY ONE *to see corruption.* Acts ii. 23–27.

REA. I understand that in accordance with the economy of the Divine government and the eternal principles of rectitude, which exist in the Divine mind, and are developed in his administration of the affairs of the universe, it was impossible that the body of Jesus should see corruption. And it appears, also, that, although Christ died, yet he was not, judicially, as fallen man is, under the bond or sentence of death. The penalty, "Dust thou art, and unto dust thou shalt return," could have no bearing upon him: and consequently he could not be retained under the dominion of death. Was then his death voluntary? and had he power to assume life again?

REV. Jesus said, Therefore doth my Father love me, *because* I LAY DOWN MY LIFE THAT I MIGHT TAKE IT AGAIN. No man taketh it from me, but I lay it down of MYSELF. I HAVE POWER TO LAY IT DOWN *and* I HAVE POWER TO TAKE IT AGAIN. This commandment have I received of my Father. John x. 17, 18. For as the Father hath life in himself, so hath he given to the Son to have life in himself. John v. 26.

REA. In these passages Christ evidently speaks of himself as the Son of God, and the only Mediator between God and man, and declares that his death and rising again were acts of his own, *voluntary* and *designed;* and effected in accordance with his Father's will, and in virtue of a power and principle of life which the Father had given him. Has he elsewhere said any thing to the same purpose?

Rev. Jesus answered and said to them, Destroy this temple, and in three days *I will raise it up*. But he spake of the temple of his *body*. When therefore he was risen from the dead, his disciples remembered that he had said this unto them; and they believed the Scriptures, and the words which Jesus had said. John ii. 19-22.

Rea. It certainly was impossible, in accordance with the Divine economy, that the body of Jesus should see corruption. Did it then differ any from the natural bodies of mankind generally?

Rev. And the angel said unto her, Fear not, Mary, for thou hast found favor with God. And, behold, thou shalt conceive in thy womb, and bring forth a son, and shalt call his name JESUS. He shall be *great*, and shall be called the *Son of the Highest;* and the Lord God shall give unto him the throne of his father David: and he shall reign over the house of Jacob *forever*, and of his kingdom *there shall be no end*. Then Mary said unto the angel, How shall this be, seeing I know not a man? And the angel answered and said unto her, *The Holy Spirit shall come upon thee,* even* *the power of the Highest shall overshadow thee;* therefore also that HOLY ONE† *who shall be born of thee, shall be called the* SON OF GOD. Luke i. 30-35. Now

---

* The Greek καὶ has frequently the sense of *even*, and I think it has that sense in this place.

† There is no word in the Greek corresponding with *thing*. It makes better sense by supplying the term ONE.

all this was done, that it might be fulfilled which was spoken of the Lord by the prophet, saying, Behold, a VIRGIN shall be with child, and shall bring forth a son, and they shall call his name EMMANUEL, which being interpreted is, GOD WITH US. Mat. i. 22, 23.

REA. From this it appears that the conception of Jesus Christ was not according to natural generation; but was effected by the Divine Spirit in a supernatural and inconceivable manner. Hence the son of Mary was truly the Son of God incarnated. Did not his incarnation, and being born of a woman, involve him in the sin of the first representative man, and subject him to death as the penalty of that sin?

REV. And ye know that he was manifested to take away our sins; and in him is no sin. 1 John iii. 5. For such a high priest became us, who is *holy, harmless, undefiled,* SEPARATE FROM SINNERS, and made higher than the heavens. Heb. vii. 26. *Who did no sin,* neither was *guile* found in his mouth. 1. Pet. ii. 22. *Who knew no sin.* 2 Cor. v. 21.

REA. He must, indeed, have been holy; his nature sinless and pure; his life immaculate in word and deed; every affection of his mind and every sensation of his body so perfectly tempered as not to admit of any morbid action or the least irregular movement. How then could he sympathize with us, and to what extent be affected in our behalf?

REV. Forasmuch then as the children are partakers of *flesh and blood,* he also himself likewise took *part of the same,* that through death he might destroy him that had the power of death, that is, the devil; and deliver them, who through fear of death, were all their lifetime subject to bondage. For verily he took not on him (the form or condition) of angels; but he took on him (the form or condition) of the seed of Abraham.* Wherefore in all things it behooved him to be made *like unto his brethren*, that he might be a merciful and faithful High Priest in things pertaining to God, to make reconciliation for the sins of the people. For in that he himself hath suffered, being tempted, he is *able* to succor them that are tempted. Heb. ii. 14-18. For we have not a High Priest which *cannot be touched with the feeling of* our infirmities, but was in all points tempted like as we are, *yet without sin*. Heb. iv. 15. For consider him that *endured* such contradiction of sinners against himself, lest ye be wearied and faint in your minds. Heb. xii. 3.

REA. The incarnation of Christ was then an assumption of the condition of Abraham's seed—a being made in the likeness of sinful flesh—and was necessary to qualify him to act as Mediator between God and men; and, as High Priest of the human family, offer to God an acceptable sacrifice for the sins of the world. But, if his Divine humanity was essentially free from natural infirmity, how did he qualify himself for the work of redemption, which required sacrifice and suffering?

REV. Who, being in the *form of God*, thought it not robbery to be as God;† but *made himself of no reputation*, and took upon him the *form of a servant*, and was made in the *likeness of man;* and being found *in fashion as a man, he humbled himself*, and became obe-

---

* See Note A. † See Note B.

dient unto death, even the death of the cross. Phil. ii. 6–8. For he shall grow up before him as a tender plant, and as a root out of a dry ground: he hath no *form nor comeliness;* and when we shall see him, there is no beauty that we should desire him. He is despised and rejected of men; a man of sorrows, and acquainted with grief: and we hid, as it were, our faces from him; he was despised, and we esteemed him not. Surely he hath borne *our* griefs, and carried *our* sorrows: yet we did esteem him stricken, smitten of God, and afflicted. But he was wounded for *our* transgressions, he was bruised for *our* iniquities: the chastisement of *our* peace was upon him; and with his stripes we are healed. Isa. liii. 2–5. Himself *took our infirmities and bare our sicknesses.* Matt. viii. 17.

REA. It appears, then, that though he was not personally liable to disease or pain or death, yet he could voluntarily suffer, in accordance with the will of God, and actually endured affliction, and sorrow, and death, for the reconciliation of transgressors. But he could not suffer any thing beyond what was included in his mediatorial work; and hence was not liable to corruption, which was not included in the things he had to endure; and had it been so ordained that he should have remained longer in the sepulchre, still his body would not have decayed. But he would have preserved his flesh from corruption by the same power by which he rose again from the dead. What amazing grace! The Son of God who dwelt in the bosom of the Father vailed his glory, divested himself of the form or condition of Godhead which he had with the Father before the world was; and by a mysterious, but real incarnation, took the form of a servant, was made in the likeness of sinful flesh, suffered, and died for our redemption!

Rev. For ye know the grace of our Lord Jesus Christ, that, though he was rich, yet for your sakes he became poor, that ye, through his poverty, might be rich. 2 Cor. viii. 9. For he hath made him who knew no sin to be a sin-offering* for us, that we might be made the righteousness of God in him. 2 Cor. v. 21. For Christ also hath once suffered for sins, the just for the unjust, that he might bring us to God. 1 Pet. iii. 18.

Rea. This was truly a wonderful exhibition of grace, and excites in my soul the liveliest perception of the demerit of sin, which required such a sacrifice for its expiation; and I trust a saving apprehension of the mercy thus manifested in providing such a sacrifice and Saviour. Was the Divine nature and immaculate purity of Jesus Christ necessary to the acceptability and merit of his sacrifice?

Rev. Forasmuch then as ye know that ye are not redeemed with corruptible things, as silver and gold, but with the precious blood of Christ, *as of a lamb without blemish and without spot;* who verily was foreordained before the foundation of the world, but was manifest in these last times for you; who by him do believe in God that raised him up from the dead and gave him glory, that your faith and hope might be in God. 1 Pet. i. 18–21. But Christ being come a High Priest of good things to come, by a greater and more

---

* See Note C.

perfect tabernacle not made with hands, that is to say, not of this building; neither by the blood of goats and calves, but by his own blood, he entered in once into the holy place, having obtained eternal redemption for us. For if the blood of bulls and of goats, and the ashes of a heifer, sprinkling the unclean, sanctifieth to the purifying of the flesh; how much more shall the blood of Christ, who, through the eternal Spirit, offered himself *without spot to God*, purge your conscience from dead works to serve the living God? Heb. ix. 11–14.

Rea. The sacrifices here alluded to undoubtedly indicated, typically, the unblemished nature and immaculate character of Jesus Christ, who is called the Lamb of God that taketh away the sins of the world. And they show that none but a pure and perfect sacrifice would be acceptable to God. The tabernacle in which Christ served was the heavenly; and the heavenly things had to be purified with a better sacrifice than was ordained for the earthly tabernacle which Moses pitched in the wilderness. O how wonderful that that sacrifice should be his own body; and that he should enter into the Holiest of all with his own blood, having obtained eternal redemption for us! O how sweet are thy words unto me! Hast thou any further testimony concerning the Divine nature of Jesus?

Rev. *In the beginning* was the Word, and the Word was *with* God, and the Word *was* God. The same was in the beginning *with* God. All things were made by him; and *without* him was not any thing made that is made. John i. 1–3. And the Word was

13*

made Flesh and dwelt among us, (and we beheld his glory, the glory as of the only begotten of the Father,) full of grace and truth. John i. 14. For in him dwelleth all the fullness of the Godhead bodily. Col. ii. 9.

Rea. I understand, then, that Jesus Christ who dwelt among men in a state of humiliation is the Word, the Son of God, who was with God before the world was, and *by whom* God made the worlds; who, also, being the brightness of his glory and express image of his person appeared as God, in the ages previous to his incarnation, and *represented* God.* I also learn that the incarnation changed the condition of his being, but not the essence of his nature.

The Word *made* Flesh was

" As much when in the manger laid,
 Almighty Ruler of the sky,
As when the six days' work he made
 Filled all the morning stars with joy."—Watts.

Am I not then to understand that the Word made Flesh is substantially and essentially the same in his incarnate condition that he was before his incarnation, and indeed that he was in the beginning with God?

Rea. That which was from *the beginning,* which we have *heard,* which we have *seen with our eyes,* which we have *looked upon,* and *our hands have handled* of the Word of Life;† (for the Life was manifested, and

---

* See Note D.

† The Greek περι του λογου της ζωης perhaps would be better rendered " *concerning the* Word the living One," or " *concerning the* Living Word."—See Macknight *in loco.*

we have *seen it*, and bear witness, and show unto you THAT ETERNAL LIFE, which was *with the* FATHER, and was manifested unto us;) THAT which we have seen and heard declare we unto you, that ye also may have fellowship with us; and truly our fellowship is with the FATHER, and with his SON JESUS CHRIST. 1 John i. 1–3.

REA. Then it was indeed the LIVING WORD who was in the beginning with God, whom they heard, and saw, and looked upon, and handled. But they could not see and look upon and handle an invisible and intangible spirit. Hence the LIVING WORD was the *Son of God made flesh*, and who really existed *in the beginning*. Am I not correct in my conception of the substantial identity of the *man Christ Jesus* and the *Living Word* who, as the PERSONAL WISDOM, says, (Prov. viii. 22–31,) The Lord possessed me in the beginning of his way, before his works of old. I was set up from everlasting, from the beginning, or ever the earth was. When there were no depths, I was brought forth, etc.

REV. Wherefore he saith, When he ascended up on high, he led captivity captive, and gave gifts unto men. (Now that he ascended, what is it but that he also *descended first* into the lower parts of the earth? He that descended is the SAME also that ascended up far above all heavens, that he might fill all things.) Eph. iv. 8–10. No man hath ascended up to heaven, but he that came down from heaven, even the Son of man who is in heaven. John iii. 13. Jesus Christ the SAME yesterday, and to-day, and forever. Heb. xiii. 8

REA. This is truly an astonishing contemplation!

The LIVING WORD who was *in the beginning* with GOD and *represented* GOD, by *appearing as* GOD, was incarnated, was heard, seen, looked upon, and handled; and was the SAME when in the flesh that he was *in the beginning* with GOD; the SAME that he *now is* and *ever shall be*. Dr. A. Clarke was of opinion that the rudiments of the human nature of Christ was a *real creation* in the womb of the Virgin, by the energy of the Spirit of God :* and it is commonly received that there are two natures in Christ ; one Divine, self-existent, unoriginated ; the other human, dependent and originated, according to Dr. Clarke's opinion, about 1860 years ago. But I now perceive that these views cannot be correct; for they could not see, look upon, and handle the supposed Divine nature, that being invisible and intangible ; and if the supposed human nature was originated only 1860 years ago, then it could not have been in the beginning with God, and could not have first descended from heaven before it ascended up to heaven. But thy anointing, O blessed Revelation, teaches me that Jesus Christ is the WORD that was in the beginning with God, and was mysteriously incarnated, and dwelt with men, being seen and handled by them, thus affording infallible proof that he had assumed the condition of those whom he came to save. Is not this what you would have me believe ?

REV. Jesus said unto them, Verily, verily, I say unto you, Moses gave you not that bread from heaven; but my Father giveth you the true bread from heaven. *For*

---

* See Dr. A. Clarke's Com. on Matt. i. 20 and Luke i. 35.

the bread of God is HE *who cometh down from heaven, and giveth life unto the world.* John vi. 32, 33. *I am the* LIVING BREAD *which came down from heaven; if any man eat of this bread, he shall live forever; and the bread that I will give is* MY FLESH, *which I will give for the life of the world.* (v. 51.) *This is the bread which came down from heaven; not as your fathers did eat manna and are dead: he that eateth of this bread shall live forever.* (v. 58.) *Verily, verily, I say unto you, He that believeth on me hath everlasting life. I am that bread of life.* (vv. 47, 48.)

REA. Truly Jesus said that HIS FLESH was the bread which came down from heaven, and this agrees not with, and disproves the opinion of those who hold that though the Spirit of Jesus was created or begotten before all things, and was with God in the beginning; yet his body was originated in the womb of the Virgin, about 1860 years ago. The term *The Word was made flesh* imports that the Divine humanity was incarnated—and that his substance or essence was the same after incarnation as before. The phrase "a body hast thou prepared me," has reference to the condition which the Divine humanity, by the power of the Highest, assumed through the medium of the Virgin, and does not refer to any *new creation.* It is evident that Jesus taught the Jews that he, himself, whom they heard and saw and looked upon; he, himself, the incarnate WORD, who stood before them in the flesh; he, himself, came down from heaven to give life unto the world; and that they must believe in him to obtain everlasting life. Hence he said, Whoso eateth my flesh and drinketh my blood hath eternal life: and I will raise him up at the last day. For my flesh is meat indeed, and my blood is drink indeed." He thus proposes the doctrine of the incarnation as an essential one. And shows that without faith in him as the WORD made FLESH, as the manifested Son of God they had no life, that is, no eternal life. Is it not so?

REV. And he said unto them, *Ye are from beneath;* I AM FROM ABOVE; *Ye are of this world;* I AM NOT OF THIS WORLD. I said therefore unto you, that ye shall die in your sins; *for if ye believe not that* I AM He, ye shall die in your sins. Then said they unto him, Who art thou? And Jesus saith unto them, Even the same that I said unto you from the beginning. John viii. 23–25. *I proceeded forth and came from God;* neither came I of myself, but he sent me. (v. 42.) Hereby know ye the Spirit of God. Every spirit that confesseth *that Jesus Christ is come in the flesh*, is of God: and every spirit that confesseth not that Jesus Christ is come in the flesh, is not of God: and this is that spirit of anti-christ whereof ye have heard that it should come; and even now already is it in the world. 1 John iv. 2, 3. Wherefore I give you to understand that no man speaking by the Spirit of God calleth Jesus accursed; and that no man can say that JESUS IS THE LORD, but by the Holy Spirit. 1 Cor. xii. 3. The first man (Adam) is of the earth, earthy; *the second man* (Christ) *is the* LORD *from heaven.* 1 Cor. xv. 47.

REA. Jesus certainly spake of himself as the incarnated WORD, as the one whom they heard, and saw, and looked upon, and handled. He did not say, I have a human nature like your own which is from beneath, and is *very man;* but I have also a Divine nature which is from above, and is *very God.* He makes the assertion that he, *himself*, whom they saw and conversed with, was *from above;* that he *proceeded* and *came forth from God.* It is the *second man*, not the second person of a tri-personal God, who is the LORD from heaven. Is not the denial of this great truth a mark and characteristic of anti-christ?

REV. Who is a liar, but he that denieth that Jesus is the Christ? He is anti-christ that denieth the Father and the Son. Whosoever denieth the Son, the same hath not the Father; but he that acknowledgeth the Son, hath the Father also. Let that therefore abide in you which you have heard from the beginning. If that which ye have heard from the beginning shall remain in you, ye also shall continue in the Son and in the Father. 1 John ii. 22-24.

REA. Then he that says that Jesus is "a mere man," and he that says that Jesus was " a *new creation* in the womb of the Virgin," deny that Jesus is the Son of God; both make him a creature; both deny his pre-existence; both make his existence to commence with his conception in the womb of the Virgin; both deny that he is the Son of God by whom all things were created. And denying the Son, they have not the Father. The Father is revealed only through the Son. Am I not correct?

REV. Jesus answered, Ye neither know me nor my Father; if ye had known me ye should have known my Father also. John viii. 19. All things are delivered unto me of my Father; and no man knoweth the Son but the Father; neither knoweth any man the Father, save the Son, and he to whomsoever the Son will reveal him. Mat. xi. 27. No man hath seen God at any time; the only-begotten Son, who is in the bosom of the Father, he hath declared him. John i. 18. Jesus saith unto him, I am the way, the truth, and the life; no man cometh unto the Father, but by me. If ye had known me, ye should have known my Father also; and from henceforth ye know him and have seen him. Philip saith unto him, Lord, show us the Father, and it sufficeth us. Jesus saith unto him, Have I been so long time with you, and yet hast thou not known me, Philip? He that hath seen me hath seen the Father; and how sayest thou then Show us the Father? Believest thou not that I am in the Father, and the Father in me? the words that I speak unto you I speak not of myself; but the Father that dwelleth in me, he doth the works. Believe me that I am in the Father and the Father in me; or else believe me for the very works' sake. John xiv. 6–11.

Rea. I understand that God is a Spirit, everywhere present but invisible, and no man hath seen him at any time. The Son of God is the revealer of the Godhead; and the theophanies of the old dispensations were manifestations of God through the Son, who being in the form of God thought it no robbery to appear as God. And when he was incarnated, his relation as the revealer of the Godhead was not changed, though his condition was changed. He was still the representative of God, and in him the Father was manifested. Hence he could say truly, He that hath seen me, hath seen the Father; for he was still the image of the invisible God; the same yesterday and to-day, and forever. Was it not thus that God was seen in the incarnate Word?

Rev. And without controversy, great is the mystery of godliness; *God was manifested in the* FLESH, justified in the spirit, seen of angels, preached unto the gentiles, believed on in the world, received up into glory. 1 Tim. iii. 16.

Rea. I understand by this that inasmuch as the Word or Son of God who was with God in the beginning, and represented God in the ancient theophanies, *was made flesh;* so God, who is never manifested except by the Son, was by him manifested in the flesh, that is in his incarnate state.* Did Christ, during his humiliation, give any special exhibition of his glory to his disciples?

Rev. And he said unto them, Verily I say unto you, that there be some of them that stand here, which shall not taste of death, till they have seen the kingdom of God come with power. And after six days, Jesus taketh Peter, James, and John his brother, and bringeth them up into a high mountain apart, and was transfigured before them; *and his face did shine as the sun, and his raiment was white as the light.* And, behold, a bright cloud overshadowed them; and, behold, a voice out of the cloud, which said, This is my beloved Son, in whom I am well pleased; hear ye him. Mark ix. 1, and Mat. xvii. 1-5. For we have not followed cunningly devised fables, when we made known

---

* See Note E.

unto you the power and coming of our Lord Jesus Christ, but were eye-witnesses of his majesty. For he received from God the Father honor and glory, when there came such a voice to him from the excellent glory, THIS IS MY BELOVED SON, in whom I am well pleased. And this voice which came from heaven, we heard when we were with him in the holy mount. 2 Pet. i. 16–18.

REA. "It is observed that the condition in which Jesus Christ appeared among men—humble—poor—despised, was a true and continual transfiguration; whereas the transfiguration itself, in which he showed himself in the real splendor of his glory, was his true and natural condition." CRUDEN. The transfiguration appears to have been a miniature representation of the coming kingdom of Christ, when he will appear in his glory and in the glory of his Father. His condition before his incarnation was glorious, and his condition now is glorious, and his condition hereafter will be glorious; and such I take to be the real condition of Christ. His condition of humiliation and suffering was then only assumed for the purposes of human redemption.

REV. But we see Jesus, who was made a little lower than the angels for the sufferings of death, crowned with *glory* and *honor ;* that he by the grace of God should taste death for every man. Heb. ii. 9. But we speak the wisdom of God in a mystery, even the hidden wisdom which God ordained before the world unto our glory: which none of the princes of this world knew: for had they known it, they would not have crucified the *Lord of Glory.* 1 Cor. ii. 7, 8.

REA. I am led to the conclusion that the Divine humanity of Christ was really in itself most glorious and perfect, and had he not vailed it in a humble condition by taking upon him the form of a servant, his brightness would have shone forth with such a splendor as would have overpowered mortal vision.

> " Behold the Lamb of God, who bears
> The sins of all the world away!
> A servant's lowly form he wears,
> He sojourns in a house of clay!
> His GLORY *is no longer seen*,
> But God with God is man with men."—WESLEY.

If this is so, and I see nothing to the contrary, may not the body of Christ have been in the days of his humiliation constituently spiritual and incorruptible?

REV. And so it is written, The first man Adam was made a *living soul;* and the last Adam was made a QUICKENING SPIRIT. Howbeit that was not first which is spiritual, but that which is natural; and afterward that which is spiritual. The first man is of the earth earthy; the SECOND MAN IS THE LORD FROM HEAVEN. As is the earthy, such are they also that are earthy; and as is the heavenly, such are they also that are heavenly. And as we have borne the image of the earthy, we also bear the image of the heavenly. Now this I say, that flesh and blood cannot inherit the kingdom of God; neither doth corruption inherit incorruption. Behold I show you a mystery: We shall not all sleep, but we shall all be changed, in a moment, in the twinkling of an eye, at the last trump;

for the trumpet shall sound, and the dead shall be raised *incorruptible*, and we shall be changed. For this corruptible must put on incorruption, and this mortal must put on immortality. 1 Cor. xv. 45–59.

REA. I perceive the argument of the apostle is, that the body of Christ was constituently a spiritual and incorruptible body, inasmuch as he was the Lord from heaven; and that believers in Christ who by nature inherit a mortal and corruptible body from the first Adam, shall eventually be changed into the image of Christ; that this change shall take place at the last day, when the trump of God shall sound; and then the body of Christ will be the pattern after which the bodies of all the saints shall be constituted, also spiritual and incorruptible. Is it not so?

REV. For our polity* is in heaven; from whence also we look for the Saviour, the Lord Jesus Christ; who shall change our vile body, that it may be fashioned like unto his glorious body, according to the working whereby he is able even to subdue all things to himself. Phil. iii. 20, 21.

REA. It appears then that it was the Incarnate Word, the Son of God, who really suffered on the cross, was buried and rose again the third day. Hence the sacrifice offered for our sins was not the death of a mere man like ourselves; nor of one whose "human nature was a real creation in the womb of the Virgin;" but it was the *death of the Son of God* himself, and therefore a DIVINE SACRIFICE of infinite merit on which we may confidently rely as trust-

---

* See Note F.

worthy ground of pardon and acceptance with God. Is it not so?

Rev. Forasmuch as ye know that ye are not redeemed with *corruptible things* as silver and gold, from your vain conversation received by tradition, from your Father; but with the *precious blood* of Christ, as of a lamb without blemish and without spot. Who verily was *foreordained before the foundation of the world*, but was MANIFEST *in these last times* for you, who by him do believe in God that raised him up from the dead, and gave him glory; that your faith and hope might be in God. 1 Pet. i. 18–21. For I delivered unto you first of all that which I also received, how that Christ died for our sins according to the Scriptures; and that he was buried, and that he rose again the third day according to the Scriptures; and that he was seen of Cephas, then of the twelve; after that he was seen of above five hundred brethren at once. After that he was seen of James; then of all the apostles. 1 Cor. xv. 3–7. To whom also he showed himself alive after his passion, by many infallible proofs, being seen of them forty days, and speaking of the things pertaining to the kingdom of God. Acts i. 3. And he led them out as far as to Bethany; and he lifted up his hands and blessed them. And it came to pass while he blessed them, he was parted from them, and carried up into heaven. And they worshiped him and returned to Jerusalem with great joy. Luke xxiv. 50–52.

Rea. The present condition of Jesus, then, is what may be considered as the natural condition of his Divine humanity—a condition which belongs to him as the Son of God, and which he had before his incarnation.

Rev. In the year that king Uzziah died, I saw also the Lord sitting upon a throne, high and lifted up, and his train filled the temple. Above it stood the seraphim; each one had six wings; with twain he covered his face, and with twain he covered his feet, and with twain he did fly. And one cried unto another and said, Holy, holy, holy is the Lord of hosts; the whole earth is full of his glory. Also I heard the voice of the Lord saying, Whom shall I send, and who will go for us? Then said I, Here am I, send me. And he said, Go, and tell this people, Hear ye indeed, but understand not; and see ye indeed, but perceive not. Make the heart of this people fat, and make their ears heavy, and shut their eyes; lest they see with their eyes, and hear with their ears, and understand with their heart, and convert, and be healed. Isa. vi. 1–3, 8–10. These things said Esaias *when he saw his glory and spake of him.* John xii. 41.

Rea. It was then our Lord Jesus Christ, the image (representative) of the invisible God, who was seen by Isaiah as you have described. But when he was incarnated he laid aside or vailed that glory, and became a man of sorrows and acquainted with grief. Did he make any manifestation of his resumption of that glory after his ascension into heaven?

Rev. And I turned to see the voice that spake with me. And being turned, I saw seven golden candlesticks; and in the midst of the seven candlesticks, *one like unto the Son of man,* clothed with a garment down to his feet, and girt about the paps with a golden girdle. His head and his hairs were white like wool, as white as snow: and his eyes were as a flame of fire: and his feet like unto fine brass, as if it burned in a furnace: and his voice as the sound of many waters. And he had in his right hand seven stars, and out of his mouth went a sharp two-edged sword: and his countenance was as the sun shining in his strength. And when I saw him, I fell at his feet as dead. And he laid his right hand upon me, saying unto me, Fear not; I AM THE FIRST AND THE LAST; I AM HE THAT LIVETH, AND WAS DEAD; AND BEHOLD I AM ALIVE FOREVER MORE, Amen, and have the keys of hell and of death. Rev. i. 12–18.

REA. Is not Jesus Christ the Messenger Jehovah, who being in the form of God appeared as God to the patriarchs and prophets of old?

REV. Jesus answered, If I honor myself, my honor is nothing: It is my Father that honoreth me, of whom ye say, hat the is your God: yet ye have not known him: and if I should say, I know him not, I shall be a liar like unto you: but I know him, and keep his saying. Your father Abraham rejoiced to see my day: and he saw it, and was glad. Then said the Jews unto him, Thou art not yet fifty years old, and hast thou seen Abraham? Jesus said unto them, Verily, verily, I say unto you, BEFORE ABRAHAM WAS I AM. John viii. 54–58.

REA. What is the testimony of God concerning the pre-existence and Divine nature of the Lord Jesus Christ?

REV. And thou Bethlehem Ephratah, though thou be little among the thousands of Judah, yet *out of thee shall he come forth unto me* that is to be Ruler in Israel; *whose goings forth have been from of old, from everlasting.* Mic. v. 2. But unto the Son he saith, Thy throne, O God, is forever and ever; a sceptre of righteousness is the sceptre of thy kingdom: Thou hast loved righteousness and hated iniquity; therefore, GOD, even THY GOD, hath anointed thee with the oil of gladness above thy fellows. And, thou Lord in the beginning hast laid the foundation of the earth, and the heavens are the work of thy hands: they shall perish, but thou remainest; and they shall wax old as doth a garment; and as a vesture shalt thou fold them up; and they shall be changed; but thou art the same, and thy years shall not fail. Heb. i. 8–12.

REA. It appears then, that Jesus, who came forth out of Bethlehem by being made of a woman, was the same whose goings forth were of old from everlasting as the Son of God. That by him God created all things and upholds and governs all. That he sustained the character of the Messenger Jehovah, and to the patriarchs and prophets in old times appeared as God, and was called by the names of God. Is it not so?

REV. For unto us a Child is born, unto us a Son is given, and the government shall be upon his shoulder; and his name shall be called Wonderful, Counselor, The Mighty God, The everlasting Father, The Prince of Peace. Isa. ix. 6.*

REA. O what a blessed light breaks in upon my soul! My Saviour is revealed to me in his Divine hu-

---

* See Note G.

manity, and with Thomas I exclaim, "My Lord, and my God!" I ask no more.

> I know thee now thou HOLY ONE,
> For thee I face to face have seen—
> The WORD Divine made *flesh*, I own
> As God with God, as man with men.

I now perceive the nature and character of my blessed Lord and Saviour. The Word is made flesh—the Son of God is made of a woman, is made in the likeness of men; but, being Adam's Creator and Lord, he was not involved in the condemnation of Adam's sin, consequently it was impossible for his body to see corruption, and it would not have undergone the temporary death to which it was not naturally liable, had it not been voluntarily for the purpose of making an atonement for sin, and reconciling us to God. It is therefore impossible that the Divine humanity of our Lord could be subject to corruption: for though it was possible that the spirit and body might be separated for a time, it was not liable to dissolution, inasmuch as it was not a natural body but a spiritual body. And as the Father has life in himself, even so he gave to the Son to have life in himself. I see Jesus thus fully qualified by the dignity of his nature as the only-begotten Son of God, the spotless purity of his character and his voluntary sufferings, for the great work of man's redemption. My Great High Priest and sacrifice is the Son of God; and with Watts I exclaim,

> "A guilty, weak and helpless worm
> Into thine arms I fall;
> Be thou my strength and righteousness,
> My Jesus and my all."

Blessed Revelation! I wonder at the glorious things thou hast made known unto me. The law of thy mouth is better unto me than thousands of gold and silver.

Rev. All the words of my mouth are in righteousness; there is nothing froward or perverse in them. They are all plain to him that understandeth, and right to them that find knowledge. Receive my instructions and not silver, and knowledge rather than choice gold. Prov. viii. 8–10. The Lord Jesus Christ be with thy spirit. 2 Tim. iv. 22.

Rea. Amen.

NOTES.

A.

Heb. ii. 16. I regard this sentence as elliptical. Parkhurst, I think, gives the true meaning of the verb ἐπιλαμβανω in this place, viz., *to assume—to take upon one.* See his Lexicon. The verb is compounded of ἐπι *upon* and λαμβανω *to take.* Λαμβανω is used in Phil. ii. 7, in this sense, and ἐπι in construction only strengthens this meaning or intensifies it. But as the verb *take* is equivalent to the meaning given by Parkhurst, we may, marking the ellipses, translate the sentence thus, "For truly he took not ——— of angels, but he took ——— of the seed of Abraham." The ellipsis in each member of the sentence should be filled with the same word properly to express the apostle's meaning. It should be one significant of something belonging to both angels and Abraham's seed. What it is must be learned from the apostle's argument, in accordance with the analogy of faith, corroborated by other parallel passages of Scripture. King James' translators supplied the first ellipsis with the word *nature* and left the second unsupplied; but if the genitive αγγελων required that some word should be supplied to complete the sense of the first member of this sentence, the genitive σπερματος required the same for the second, which is as evidently elliptical as the first. The word *nature*, however, does not accord with the apostle's argument, which relates to the Saviour's condition of humiliation and suffering. The word *nature* relates to the essence or substance of a thing; but the apostle is not speaking of the being or substance of Christ, but of what he took upon him; hence the term *nature* is inappropriately, if not absurdly, used in this case. It does not agree with other Scriptures, which speak of Christ as being made in the *likeness* of men and being found in *fashion* as a man, and as taking on him *the form of a servant*, etc. Nor is it in accordance with the analogy of faith, which represents Christ as a Divine person, a quickening Spirit, and not a natural man.

In the revised version by the American Bible Union the passage is thus rendered, "For surely he doth not help angels, but he helpeth the seed of Abraham." This rendering appears objectionable on the following grounds:

1st. Some Scriptures import that Christ does help angels. Compare Matt. xxviii. 18; Luke xix. 38; Eph. i. 10; iii. 15; Phil. ii. 10; Col. i. 20.

2d. That his help is not restricted to Abraham's seed only, whether the natural seed or the seed of faith, but extends to all mankind to some degree. 1 Tim. ii. 1–7, and iv. 10.

3d. There does not appear to be any reference to

fallen angels in this discourse of the apostle's In chap. i. 4, 5, 6, 7, 13, 14, and ii. 2, 5, 7, 9, the reference is to the holy angels, and without doubt they are still the subjects of discourse in v. 16, which therefore requires a corresponding signification. The meaning imposed by this rendering upon the apostle's language is altogether foreign to his argument, which is to show that Jesus Christ was made a little lower than the angels for the suffering of death; and made *like* his brethren, that he might be a merciful and faithful High Priest in things pertaining to God, to make reconciliation for the sins of the people.

The word *condition* (or *form*, in the sense of condition, as used in Phil. ii. 7,) is unobjectionable and no doubt the right one. It makes good sense, accords with the apostle's argument, is scriptural, and agrees with the analogy of faith. Phil. ii. 6–8 is, I think, a parallel passage with Heb. ii. 16–18, and from it I would supply the ellipses in this sentence by the word μορφη, *form* or *condition*, and render it thus, "For truly he took not the condition of angels, but he took the condition of Abraham's seed." It was thus that he qualified himself for the work of human redemption by taking a condition lower than that of the angels, even the condition of fallen humanity.

B.

Phil. ii. 6–8. Dr. Doddridge translates this passage thus: "Let the same mind be in you which was also in Christ Jesus, who, being in the form of God, thought it not robbery to be as God, nevertheless, emptied himself, taking upon him the form of a servant, when made in the likeness of men: and being found in fashion as a man, he humbled himself, becoming obedient even unto death, death of the cross." On the clause ισα Θεω, which he paraphrases "*to be* and appear *as God*," he says, "So ισα Θεω is most exactly rendered, agreeable to the force of ισα in many places in the *Septuagint*, which Dr. Whitby has collected in his *note* on this place. The proper Greek phrase for *equal to God* is ισον τω Θεω, which is used John v. 18.

Macknight renders it thus, "Who being in the form of God, did not think it robbery *to be like God*," and says, "so το ειναι ισα Θεω literally signifies." For Whitby hath proved in the clearest manner, that ισα is used adverbially by the LXX to express *likeness*, but not *equality*, the proper term for which is ισον. So that if the apostle had meant to say *equal with God*, the phrase would have been ισον Θεω as we have in John v. 18.

The phrase *form of God* is evidently used to designate the pre-existent state of Christ, and the *form of a servant* is employed to express his incarnated state. These two conditions are put in antithesis, and both are predicated of the same person; but he could not sustain both at the same time. The form of God was laid aside when he took the form of a servant. Form cannot signify nature; for he could not divest himself of his nature. The form of God refers to the glory he possessed as the representative of the invisible God. Being the brightness of his glory, and the express image of his person, he thought it no robbery to be as God, and hence to the angels appeared as God, and also to the patriarchs and prophets of olden times. In this he did not rob God of the honor due him, for being the representative of God, it was his right, by the ordination of God himself, to receive adoration from those intelligences whom God had made by him. Indeed Christ himself says, "The Father judgeth no man, but hath committed all judgment to the Son, that all men should honor the Son, even as they honor the Father. He that honoreth not the Son, honoreth not the Father who hath sent him." John v. 22, 23. The claim of Christ to divine honors is not founded upon his *being God* but upon his *being in the form of God*. Being in *the form of God* he thought it no robbery to *be as God*. To be as God indicated his appearing in Godlike majesty and receiving divine honors. And this he did before he was incarnated. And yet though that was his real and proper condition as the Son of God; he did not hesitate, for the accomplishment of human redemption, to divest himself of that glory, and to make himself of no reputation, taking the form of a servant, and humbling himself even to suffer a most painful and ignominious death. Such was the greatness and extent of his love for us.

C.

2 Cor. v. 21. Dr. Barnes says, "The Greek here is, 'for him who knew no sin, he hath made sin or a sin-offering for us.' That it means that God made him (Christ) a sin-offering, is adopted by Whitby, Dodridge, Macknight, Rosenmüller and others. There are many passages in the Old Testament where the word sin' (αμαρτια) is used in the sense of sin-offering, or

a sacrifice for sin. Thus Hos. iv. 8: 'They eat up the sin of my people;' *i. e.* the sin-offerings. See Ezek. xliii. 22, 25; xliv. 29; xlv. 22, 23, 25."

Dr. A. Clarke says, "It signifies *a sin-offering* or *sacrifice for sin* and answers to the *chatuah* and *chataath* of the Hebrew text, which signifies both *sin* and *sin-offering* in a great variety of places in the Pentateuch. The *Septuagint* translate the Hebrew word by αμαρτια in ninety-four places in *Exodus, Leviticus* and *Numbers,* where a sin-offering is meant; and where our version translates the word not *sin,* but an *offering for sin.*"

D.

THE WORD REPRESENTED GOD. That this is the meaning of the clause "and the Word was God" in John i. 1, I think is unquestionable. In the preceding clause, "and the Word was with God," a distinction is made between the Word and God, corresponding to that which is made by the Saviour himself in his prayer, John xvii. 5, "And now, O Father, glorify thou me with thine ownself with the glory which I had with thee before the world was." Christ, the Word, was with God, and could not be that God with whom he was. To assert this would be contradictory and absurd. We may then inquire whether the language may not bear another and consistent meaning. D. A. Clarke says, "There is scarcely a more common form of speech in any language than *This* is, for *this* REPRESENTS or *signifies.*" And he says " *This bread* IS *my body,* has no other meaning than, *This bread* REPRESENTS *my body.*" In like manner he shows that, *This cup* IS *my blood,* means *This cup* REPRESENTS *my blood;*

and *That Rock* WAS *Christ*, signifies *That Rock* RE-PRESENTED *Christ*. Doddridge paraphrases to the same purport, and Dr. Barnes says, "*This is my body*. This represents my body. This *could not* be intended to mean that that bread was literally his body. It was not." Again, "*For this is my blood*. This *represents* my blood, as the bread did his body." Now as in these cases we avoid the absurdity of supposing the bread to be the body of Christ, and the cup the blood of Christ, and the rock in the wilderness to be really Christ himself, by giving to the verb a meaning which is very common and in accordance with the genius of all languages; so in the explanation of John i. 1, we avoid the absurdity of supposing that the Word is the God that he was with, by giving to the verb this very same meaning. "In the beginning was the Word, and the Word was with God, and the Word represented God." And this agrees with v. 18. "No man hath seen God at any time; the only-begotten Son, who is in the bosom of the Father, he hath declared him."

E.

1 Tim. iii. 16. It can scarcely be doubted, I think, that the Son of God is the person here spoken of as having been manifest in the flesh, justified in the spirit, etc. The term God is, according to both the Old and New Testaments, applied to the Son. Thus in Isa. ix. 6. "Unto us a Child is born, unto us a Son is given, and the government shall be upon his shoulder; and his name shall be called Wonderful, Counselor, Mighty God," etc. And in Heb. i. 8; "But

15*

unto the Son he saith, Thy throne, O God, is forever and ever," etc. The term God appears to have been an official designation, and employed to denote a divinely appointed messenger or ruler. Thus of Moses God said, "See, I have made thee a God to Pharaoh." The congregation of Israel are called Gods in Psalm lxxxii., because to them the word of the Lord came in the promise that they should be to him a kingdom of priests on condition of their keeping his covenant. "God standeth in the congregation of the mighty: he judgeth among the Gods," v. 1. But in consequence of their breaking his covenant, he says in vv. 6, 7. "I have said, Ye are Gods; and all of you are children of the Most High; but ye shall die like men, and fall like one of the princes." Now if Moses be called God, and if he called them Gods to whom the word of GOD came, why may not the Son of God, who is the only proper representative of God, and the heir of all things, be called God; as he is in the eighth verse of the same Psalm, "Arise, O God, judge the earth; for thou shalt inherit all nations." Hence then to say, God was manifest in the flesh, amounts to no more than that Christ the Son of God was incarnated. But as he is the representative of God, I have supposed the term God to be taken in its highest sense to denote the self-existent and invisible One—the Great Supreme, and have given the passage a meaning it will very well bear in accordance with the analogy of faith, viz., that the Supreme God was manifested in the incarnated Word.

F.

Phil. iii. 20. "For our polity is in heaven," etc. The word πολειτυμα, which the King James's translators have rendered by *conversation*, properly signifies the *administration, government*, or *polity* of a kingdom or state. It is used here to designate the polity of the glorious and everlasting kingdom of Christ which is now in heaven, reserved until the coming of Christ from heaven, when it will be revealed, and when all the saints of God shall be qualified by the resurrection and translation to enter into and possess it.

G.

Isa. ix. 6. This prophecy belongs to Jesus Christ and to no other. He is the Child born and the Son given of whom the prophet speaks. All power in heaven and earth is given into his hands, and the government of the world is on his shoulder; for he shall have dominion from sea to sea and from the rivers unto the ends of the earth. The names by which he is called are expressive of some relations and conditions which he sustains in the great Mediatorial work which is committed to his hands.

How appropriate the term WONDERFUL to him who is the only-begotten Son of God, who existed with the Father before the world was, who is the brightness of his glory and express image of his person; and who was incarnated, made flesh, and dwelt among us, the Child of a virgin mother. Truly, great is the mystery of Godliness, "God manifest in the flesh." God was manifested before the incarnation by Jesus Christ who, being in the form of God, thought it no robbery to appear as God; but after the incarnation he was manifest in the flesh—in Jesus the incarnate Word. There is no relation in which we can contemplate

Christ, in which he does not sustain the character of the WONDERFUL.

Equally appropriate is the term COUNSELOR, for in him are all the treasures of wisdom and knowledge; and he, of God, is made unto us WISDOM. By him the law was given on Sinai, and by him expounded in his Sermon on the Mount. By him the great purpose of God in redemption is revealed; and he now lives in the presence of the Father to intercede for us. He is our *Advocate* with the Father, and therefore the COUNSELOR.

He is called the MIGHTY GOD (*El-gibbor*) the prevailing or conquering God. God is an official designation, and is applied to angels, to magistrates, and rulers; but it is given to Jesus Christ pre-eminently above them all, as in Heb. i. 8, 9. "But unto the Son he saith, Thy throne, O God, is forever and ever; a sceptre of righteousness is the sceptre of thy kingdom; thou hast loved righteousness and hated iniquity; therefore God, even thy God, hath anointed thee with the oil of gladness above thy fellows." He is the conquering God, because all things shall be subdued to him, and by him reconciled to the Father. And to him every knee shall bow, and every tongue shall confess that he is Lord to the glory of God the Father.

He is called, THE EVERLASTING FATHER (*abi ad*) or FATHER OF THE EVERLASTING AGE, not as some suppose because he is the Father, for that is absurd. He cannot be the Son and the Father both. But he is so called because, as the Mediator, he will reconcile all things to God, and so bring in the everlasting age or world without end, when his saints shall all be kings and priests with him, and the rest of mankind shall be subject to their government. That everlasting age will be the consummation of his mediation, the result of the work which is committed to his hands, and hence he is called the FATHER OF THE EVERLASTING AGE.

He is called the PRINCE OF PEACE, because the atonement which he hath made for our sins makes peace; and he is our Peace. And his government over the world will insure peace forever.

There is nothing absurd or contradictory in these appellations. They all belong to Christ in his Mediatorial character and relations.

INDEX

TO DIALOGUE BETWEEN REASON AND REVELATION ON THE INCORRUPTIBILITY OF THE SAVIOUR'S BODY.

	PAGE
Salutations,	141
Incorruptibility of Christ's body,	141
Christ saw no corruption,	142
Could not be holden of death,	142
Was not judicially liable to death,	143
Suffered voluntarily,	143
Had power to resume the life he laid down,	143
Was the Son of God,	144
Was holy,	145
Was incarnated,	145
Assumed man's condition for the mediatorial work,	146
Was the Incarnated WORD,	149
The same that was in the beginning with God,	150
And not a "real creation," as Dr. A. Clarke says,	152
Came down from Heaven,	153
Doctrine of the Incarnation an essential one,	154
Its denier, an antichrist,	155
Christ represents God,	156
The Transfiguration,	157
Christ a quickening spirit,	159
His death a Divine Sacrifice,	160
His condition now what it was before the Incarnation,	162
His Divine nature, etc.,	164

NOTES.

		PAGE
A.	On Heb. ii. 16,	167
B.	On Phil. ii. 6–8,	169
C.	On 2 Cor. v. 21,	171
D.	On John i. 1,	172
E.	On 1 Tim. iii. 16,	173
F.	On Phil. iii. 20,	174
G.	On Isa. ix. 6,	175

THE END.

JUST PUBLISHED BY THE AUTHOR,

DISCOURSES

ON

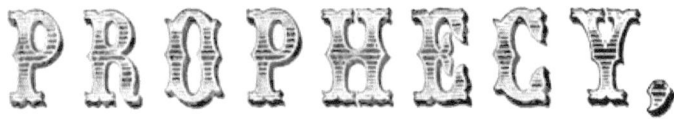

WHICH IS AS A

Light that Shineth in a Dark Place,

SHOWING THAT THE DOMINION OF THE

WILL BE GIVEN TO THE SAINTS OF GOD, AND THAT ALL THE REST OF MANKIND WILL BE SUBJECT TO THEIR GOVERNMENT.

AN INTERESTING BOOK

SECOND EDITION,

CONTAINING THE

VINDICATION OF HIS THEORY OF REDEMPTION,

406 pages, with Portrait, bound in cloth, $1.00, and will be sent, postage paid, to order, on the receipt of the price in good money or postage stamps.

Address, **JOHN G. WILSON,**
242 Hanover Street, Kensington, Philadelphia, Pa

For Notices of the Book read the following pages.

DISCOURSES ON PROPHECY.

The following notices of this book have been received from different sources.

"The author is evidently a close Bible student, and has made himself very familiar with the prophecies."—*Christian Sun.*

"The author treats the subject in a new light. The work abounds in beautiful paragraphs."—*Oxford Evening Mail.*

"It is an interesting work, characterized by an honest search after truth, and a devout spirit."—*Presbyterian.*

"The book is very readable, and none can peruse it without profit. We regard the volume as eminently calculated to do good. We recommend it to all classes as fitted to be permanently useful."—*Herald of Gospel Liberty.*

"The book is not only a book to be read, but to be thought upon."—J. N. SPOON.

"If any man takes it up, and gives his attention and thought to it, he will find what will amply repay him. He will find thought, (something scarce now-a-days,) deep, original thought. He will find logic, and most undeniable logic. He will find more and better than all that, too. He will find so much of the pure and true spirit of Christianity, that if he does not shut the book a better man, the fault is heavily his own."— * * *

"You always set me to thinking."—W. T. EVA.

"The spirit and tendency of the volume are favorable to experimental and practical piety. The author is constantly looking for Christ and his kingdom, and labors to prepare his readers to participate in the hastening glory."—T. H. STOCKTON.

"Mr. Wilson treats, in this series of discourses, of the work of Redemption, from its institution in Paradise, on the fall of our first parents, through all its steps, till Christ's triumph shall be completed over his foes. He holds to the restoration of the Israelites; the resurrection of the holy dead at the commencement of the Millennium; Christ's personal reign here: and the perpetuity of the earth, as the abode of the redeemed and the seat of his kingdom; and most of the numerous themes which he discusses are treated in a satisfactory manner. He is familiar with the sacred word; he presents his thoughts clearly, and urges them with earnestness and force."—*Theological and Literary Journal.*

"The design of this book is to show that the dominion of the world will be given to the saints of God, and that all the rest of mankind will be subject to their government. The author, who is pastor of a church in Philadelphia, is, in his manner of interpreting Scripture, what is called a Literalist; and believes that Christ will come personally before the Millennium, and with his saints will reign over the nations during that period. He also believes that the Jews, or natural seed of Abraham according to the promise, will be restored to their own land at the coming of Christ, and that the Millennium will be a mediatorial dispensation, exceeding all others in excellency and glory."—*Church Advocate.*

"Your book is written calmly and well. It displays much patient study of that side of the question."—A. WEBSTER, D.D.

"The book on prophecy has interested me more than any similar work."—H. F. MOFFATT.

'I think, without endorsing every sentiment, I can recommend the work. There is in it, obviously, originality of thought, much research, and the honest expression of the convictions of your own mind. Then the style in which you have written is decidedly good, and frequently eloquent, and your reasoning forcible, if not conclusive."—J. W. RUTLEDGE.

"Now for your book. I give you credit for great labor to find out the truth—for manly independence in making a frank and open disclosure of what you are persuaded is the truth, and for doing all this in an amiable, Christian spirit. The moral effect of your book upon the reader can't be otherwise than good—in it he will not have to sift out sand all day to get a few grains of pure gold. Contrariwise, he will find a great deal of gold, and but little sand. But still, I think, among the gold there is some sand; indeed, where is the work so full of gold as to have no sand!—God's book alone is infallible.

"I hope you will publish a second edition of your Discourses. The great events of which you have written are just at hand. The church of Christ should be roused up to investigate these subjects, and if any man believes you to be wrong, let him in the meekness of wisdom show that wrong and set you right."— GEORGE BROWN, *late President of Madison College.*

"The style is neat, and the sentiments clearly and forcibly expressed."—*Evangelical Repository.*

"The study of prophecy is one of deep interest to every man who would know what is the mind of the Spirit—one, it may be, that receives too little attention. Mr. Wilson has turned his attention largely to the study of prophecy, and has given to the world a book of much interest. He treats the prophecies in accordance with the analogy of faith, and shows in the prophetical records the unfoldings of the eternal purpose of God in the salvation of mankind by Jesus Christ. In the interpretation of scripture, Mr. Wilson may be termed a literalist, believing in the restoration of the Jews to their own land, the resurrection of the saints at the commencement of the Millennium, and the personal reign of Christ upon earth. With some of his positions we would not agree; but can, withal, cheerfully recommend the book to our readers. They will find in it *that* which many of the publications of the present day have no claim to, close, vigorous, earnest thought, and much too of the spirit of Christianity."—*Banner of the Covenant.*

www.ingramcontent.com/pod-product-compliance
Lightning Source LLC
Chambersburg PA
CBHW020238170426
43202CB00008B/135